Discoveries

From

Kurdish

Looms

Notes

𝑛

𝓇

Discoveries From Kurdish Looms is published to accompany an exhibition of the same title on view at the Mary and Leigh Block Gallery, December 9, 1983, through February 19, 1984.

Library of Congress Cataloging
in Publication Data

Main entry under title:
Discoveries from Kurdish looms.

Bibliography: p.
1. Rugs, Kurdish—Exhibitions.
I. Biggs, Robert D.
II. Mary and Leigh Block Gallery.
NK2809.K87D57 1983
746.7'5667'07401731
83-19535

ISBN 0 941680 02 9

Discoveries From Kurdish Looms is supported by funds from Northwestern University, the Mary and Leigh Block Gallery Friends of Art, The Mary and Leigh Block Endowment Fund, and a grant from the Illinois Arts Council, a State agency.

Cover: Bijar Area Village Rug, early 20th century, (detail of cat. no. 18).

Mary and Leigh Block Gallery
Northwestern University
Evanston, Illinois   60201

Discoveries

From

Kurdish

Looms

Mary and Leigh Block Gallery

Northwestern University

in conjunction with the

Chicago Rug Society

Robert D. Biggs, editor

Lenders   𝓝

      to the

Exhibition

         𝓻

R. D. Biggs

Maury Bynum

Michael Cuccello

Cynthia G. Curley

William Eagleton

Evanston Historical Society

Joseph W. Fell

McGuire Gibson

Barbara and Roger Hilpp

Michael Isberian

Sirak A. Khachikian

Mr. and Mrs. Louis C. Krueger

Mary Ann and Ian Lea

Dr. John H. Lorentz

Steve and Barbara Mackey

James McNeill Mesplé

Mr. and Mrs. Mojmir Povolny

Linda Sandell and David Schwartz

Mr. and Mrs. Wendel R. Swan

John and Suzan Wertime

Mr. and Mrs. Allen C. West

Ralph S. Yohe

Private collections

Contents

ⴖ

When the Mary and Leigh Block Gallery and the Chicago Rug Society first discussed the possibility of an exhibition of rugs and weavings, there were numerous suggestions as to what might be shown. It quickly became clear that an exhibition of Kurdish materials would be ideal; there were, in fact, several sizable collections of Kurdish weavings within the membership of the Rug Society. In addition, some Society members had firsthand experience in Kurdish areas or knew of collectors and scholars who had acquired rugs and observed Kurdish weavers in several countries of the Middle East. More important, Kurdish weaving was the only great class of Middle Eastern textiles that had not previously been given an exclusive academic exhibition.

Although Kurdish weaving does not have the uniformity displayed in the rugs of such homogeneous groups as the Turkoman, recent field work has shown that even isolated groups of Kurdish weavers employ some of the same techniques and patterns used in other Kurdish areas. Rugs and kilims that look like those of non-Kurdish neighbors still often exhibit some specifically characteristic Kurdish colors and motifs. And certain utilitarian items made by isolated Kurds not only are woven in the same way as similar pieces from the Kurdish core areas of western Iran, northern Iraq, eastern Turkey, and the Caucasus, but also may have virtually identical designs.

Some authors would argue that the weavings of the Kurds should not be grouped together due to the great variation in their design and structure. The settling of nomadic Kurds during the past century and the imposition of modern national borders dividing tribes have caused some regional differences. Over the centuries, voluntary or forced migration from the Kurdish core areas has spread the Kurds and their weavings throughout the Middle East. Some isolated Kurdish weavers have borrowed designs and techniques from their non-Kurdish neighbors, abandoning their own traditions. In addition, the Kurds, like many ethnic weavers in Iran, have taken contracts to produce rugs for the international market using non-Kurdish designs. Because of the external source of these "contract designs," some scholars are reluctant to admit town-made items such as the rugs of Senneh and Bijar to the class of Kurdish rugs, even though Kurdish women weave them and they can be distinguished by structural peculiarities from non-Kurdish rugs having similar patterns.

A latch-hooked diamond, the most typical motif in Kurdish weaving (detail of cat. no. 41).

To address such issues and to begin to define the term "Kurdish," the Block Gallery and the Chicago Rug Society have mounted an exhibition that shows a great range of Kurdish weavings from a large geographical area. Included are recent, chemically dyed, loosely woven, nomadic and village rugs along with antique masterpieces from town workshops. As this is the first exhibition to investigate solely Kurdish production, it is of prime importance to show the variety of rugs and weavings in order to make apparent the links as well as the differences between Kurdish groups. It is not so much the desire to specify what is a "Kurdish" design as it is to show that a design is used by Kurds, even if it also appears in the weavings of non-Kurdish groups. Our consideration of the technical details along with design features should enable a better determination of which rugs and weavings were, in fact, produced by the prolific Kurdish weavers of the Middle East.

Discoveries From Kurdish Looms has benefited from the scholarly contributions of the authors. Professor John R. Perry's discussion of the history of the Kurds establishes their geographic boundaries, political circumstances and cultural characteristics and serves as an important introduction. While the more commercial, workshop weavings of the towns of Senneh and Bijar could make up an entire exhibition due to their popularity in America, we have presented here only a sample of the major types within these two groups. This aspect is the subject of Murray L. Eiland's essay. Alongside these expertly woven town products, there are idiosyncratic, sometimes crudely executed, rugs from Kurdish village or nomadic looms throughout northwestern Iran. Of special significance are the Khorasani Kurdish pieces; the contributions of Amedeo de Franchis and John Wertime carry the discussion of this group far beyond the bounds of the exhibition. The inclusion of Iraqi Kurdish pieces brings to the public a type of weaving previously unknown to most rug collectors. The accompanying essay by William Eagleton provides tribal information that is rarely found in rug scholarship. Ralph Yohe's familiarity with the Kurdish weavers of Turkey provides a special dimension to his writing, enhanced by the splendid Turkish Kurdish kilims, rugs and bags.

While the strengths of the exhibition and this publication are many, it was not possible to examine or include the full geographical range and variety of Kurdish weavings. In the consideration of works for inclusion, if the provenance of a particular rug could not be assigned as the result of direct observation by the collector, by reference to documented or published examples, or through the expertise of the catalogue contributors, the piece would not be selected. Thus, a weaving attributed to the Kurds of Lebanon was omitted because we were unable to verify its origin. Several outstanding flat-woven bag faces thought to have been made by Kurdish weavers in northwestern Iran or Soviet Azerbaijan were also not chosen. Examples of the weavings of the Qazvin and Varamin area were sought, but could not be obtained. The Kurds of Khorasan should have been more broadly represented; well into the preparation of this catalogue several previously unrecognized Khorasani Kurdish rugs and bags were discovered in Chicago collections, but it was too late to include them. The research process identified other important Kurdish pieces that also were not previously recognized. These discoveries and pieces from areas still in question further illustrate the need for continued consideration of Kurdish rugs and weavings.

Finally, *Discoveries From Kurdish Looms* would not have been realized without the support and dedication of the members of the Chicago Rug Society, the staff of the Block Gallery and, most important, the generosity of the lenders. Rugs and weavings have come from as near as Evanston and as far as Baghdad; to all the lenders who have parted with pieces from their collections for a lengthy period, we express our gratitude. It is their treasures in tandem with the knowledge and insights of the catalogue contributors that have enabled us to discover the variety of weavings from Kurdish looms.

McGuire Gibson
Chicago Rug Society and
The Oriental Institute
University of Chicago

Kathy Kelsey Foley
Director
Mary and Leigh Block Gallery
Northwestern University

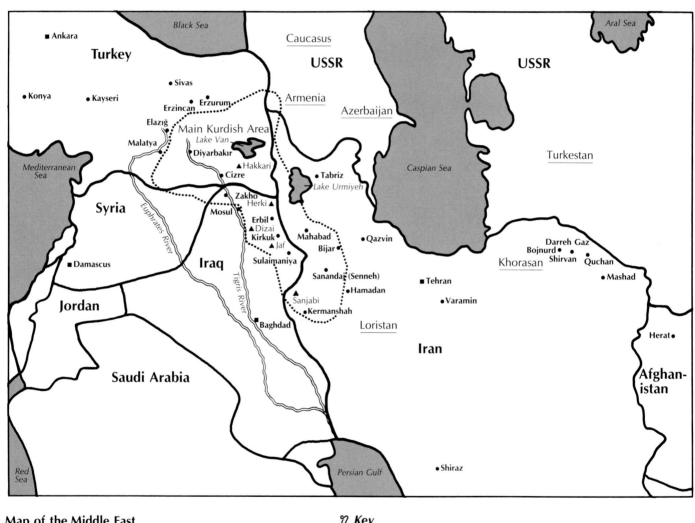

Map of the Middle East

ℜ

ℜ **Key**

— Areas
····· Main Kurdish Area
■ Capitals
● Cities
▲ Tribes

The Kurds

ᛉ

𝔫

John R. Perry

Who, What and Where?

King Solomon, who had the whole race of the jinn as his slaves, once sent 500 of them to the West with orders to seek out the 500 most beautiful virgins in Europe to add to his harem. After a long and diligent search, the jinn brought back 500 girls "as graceful and sweet as the full moon in May." Too late, for Solomon had passed on to his eternal reward in Middle Eastern folklore. The 500 jinn were each left with a fair maiden, so they married them and settled down to raise their families in a land of green hills and crystal streams in the Zagros ranges. And that, according to a popular Kurdish legend, is the origin of the Kurds.[1]

Kurdistan is a remarkable monument of human geography. It has no political existence and is not clearly defined on any side by natural topographical features. It occupies an area about 700 miles long by an average of 250 miles across, of perhaps 140,000 square miles—roughly twice the size of Syria, or almost the combined area of Indiana, Illinois and Wisconsin. Shaped like a chipped flint ax head, it lies across the mountainous adjacent frontiers of Iran, Iraq, Syria, Turkey, and Soviet Armenia and Azerbaijan. Recent estimates of the Kurdish population range from 3 to 6 million in Turkey, 2 to 4 million in Iran, 1 to 2 million in Iraq, 300,000 to 500,000 in Syria, and 80,000 to 150,000 in the Soviet Union—a total of between 7 and 13 million. We may add to this a considerable Kurdish diaspora elsewhere in the Middle East, in Europe and in America. Iran's western province known as Kurdistan comprises only a fraction of geographical Kurdistan and does not even include the majority of the Iranian Kurdish population.

There are also large Kurdish tribes in the far northeast of Iran, in the Kopet Dagh range of Khorasan, a few further north in Soviet Turkmenistan, and also in the far southeast, among the Baluch, where their ancestors were deported in thousands by vengeful shahs during the seventeenth and eighteenth centuries. In Syria and Lebanon some Kurdish groups distant from geographical Kurdistan have been assimilated into Arab communities. A good example is the chiefly families of the Jumblat Druze (Kurdish *Jān Bulāt*, "soul of steel").

What makes a Kurd? Primarily the language. Ethnically the Kurds are an Iranian people (like the Persians, the Pashtuns and the Baluch), but this sort of classification, after millennia of assimilation by migration, invasion, deportation, and intermarriage, is to a great extent a linguistic one. Culturally, too, the Kurds have been largely assimilated into the norms of the Turco-Iranian Islamic ecumene which displays a surprising uniformity of social and cultural patterns beneath the superficial variety of peoples and languages.

Their language, however, distinguishes the Kurds from all other communities within or contiguous with their domain. The various Kurdish dialects are clearly related to, though distinct from, modern Persian and the other West Iranian languages of the Indo-European family. They may be grouped into three clusters: the Northern, called Kurmanji, spoken in Turkey, Syria, the Soviet Union, and Iranian Azerbaijan; the Central group, known as Sorani, spoken in Iraq and in Iran from Mahabad to Sanandaj; and the Southern group, centered on Kermanshah. Other classifications recognize two groups, extending Kurmanji into northern Iraq and grouping the dialects of Iran and northeastern Iraq together. Two main literary languages have developed, using the Arabic alphabet and, in recent years, the Cyrillic (in the USSR) and the Latin (in Turkey and Syria) alphabets. Kurdish retains characteristic archaic Iranian features such as gender in nouns and the peculiar ergative verbal construction; but Arabic, Turkish and Persian (and to a lesser extent Armenian and Aramaic) have influenced the modern spoken and written language, chiefly by expanding its vocabulary.

An urban male Kurd in Western-style suit or shirt and flannels, with his neatly trimmed moustache and worry beads, may be physically indistinguishable from his Iranian, Turkish or Arab neighbors—though his complexion, hair and eyes are on average lighter in color. In the villages, however, the man wears a quasi-uniform costume of baggy pants gathered at the ankles and a blouse with a sash around the waist and a fringed turban (often an ''Arab'' headcloth or *keffiya* wrapped turban style); he may well be carrying a rifle and bandoleer rather than worry beads. The women—even those in towns—generally wear one or more gaily colored skirts over less voluminous trousers and a large headcloth worn scarf or turban style; they will often turn aside or draw a corner of the headscarf across the lower part of their faces in the presence of a strange man, but do not affect the Iranian *chador* or other forms of veil. There are many variations in dress according to tribe, region, age, social status, and individual whim, but the basic Kurdish attire is kept jealously distinctive as a badge of communal identity and solidarity.

The Kurds are not the only community to inhabit Kurdistan. Apart from the Arabs, Iranians and Turks (chiefly in the few cities, where they are in the majority and are increasing), there are rural communities and small urban enclaves of Assyrians (Aramaic-speaking Nestorian Christians) and other Christians; the Armenians are now chiefly found in towns (in Iran and Iraq), and the last of the Jews (Aramaic-speaking), formerly numerous in Iraq, emigrated in the 1950s. The latter at least had the ark of several disputed covenants as a lifeboat; but the Armenians and Assyrians, like the Kurds, were left high and dry when the floodwaters of world war and self-determination subsided south of Mt. Ararat. Relations between these heterogeneous neighbors have never been entirely friction-free. In a veritable cockpit of warring empires, squabbling religions and

View of the foothills of Iraqi Kurdistan; the low mound on the right is the ruins of an ancient town.

Kurdish woman spinning.

competition for scarce resources, the wonder is that their difficulties have not been much worse. The Kurds themselves, divided by tribal, regional, feudal—and, most recently, politico-ideological affiliations—have often indulged in internecine feuds that both neighboring and distant powers have been ready to exploit.

Historical Survey

The valley slopes of the western Zagros and the rolling plateau of southeastern Anatolia—sources of the Tigris and its tributaries—have yielded records of human settlement since the Paleolithic period. Sites such as Jarmo, in the Chamchamal valley, may have been where man first cultivated cereals.[2] The numerous caves in the region—some still used to shelter livestock—have revealed traces of ancient habitation and have given rise to modern tales of hidden treasure and guardian jinn.[3] A people called the Guti were raiding Babylonia from western Kurdistan around 2200 B.C. By about 1200 B.C. various Iranian tribes, including the Medes (whose kingdom embraced eastern Kurdistan), had moved into the Zagros and commenced their lengthy sparring with the regional empires. In 400 B.C., during his epic march with the Ten Thousand, Xenophon was harried through the mountain passes north of the Tigris by the Kardukhoi, who paid homage neither to Persia nor to Armenia; if their name is not indisputably the prototype of "Kurd," their behavior certainly is.

By the time of the Arab Muslim conquest of western Iran (the 640s of our era), the term "Kurd" was broadly applied to local tribes and confederations, some of them not even Iranian. It has been used equally loosely up to fairly recent times, for example, by the sixteenth century Kurdish historian Bidlisi, and in the eighteenth century by the Armenian farmers of the Isfahan region, to include the Lori and Bakhtiyari tribes south of Kurdistan proper. Just as the present-day Kurds result from an amalgamation of various pre-Iranian and Iranian peoples with an admixture of Arabs and Turks, the current precise ethnolinguistic distinction is the cumulative result of historical pressures. These were first religious, with the conversion of Iran to Shi'ite Islam in the sixteenth century and the separate administrative status of ethnoreligious minorities (the *millet* system) in the Ottoman empire; and then political, with the rise of Turkish and Arab nationalism and the traumatic redrawing of frontiers during the early years of this century. In other words, a Kurd became progressively more strictly defined—as a Sunni, not a Shi'i, Iranian hill tribesman; as a Muslim, not an Armenian, Assyrian or Jewish peasant; as a Kurd, not an assimilated Iranian, Iraqi or Turk.

During the first eight centuries of Islam, various notable individuals and local dynasties have been identified as Kurdish, such as the historian Ibn al-Athir, and the Crusaders' nemesis, Saladin, founder of the Ayyubid dynasty in Egypt and Syria. The political history of Kurdistan proper begins during the wars between the Ottoman Turks and the Safavid dynasty of Iran throughout the sixteenth to eighteenth centuries. As we have seen, the linguistic—hence to an extent the cultural and political—divisions in Kurdistan lie between north and south rather than east and west. The vacillating frontier between the Middle Eastern superpowers of their time bisected Kurdistan from north to south, thus splitting the culturally integrated strata at right angles. The object of the sultan, as of the shah, was to capture the strategic initiative by pushing this frontier to the far side of Kurdistan, by dint of subsidizing (at times replacing or even creating) tribal leaders in "his" Kurdish provinces and if necessary campaigning in alliance with these vassals, in order to intimidate their eastern or western counterparts or to force their replacement with more tractable chieftains. This resulted in the promotion of the heads of a few leading Kurdish families to the status of hereditary marchwardens and encouraged internal rivalry and the development of a feudal system which is still evident in Kurdistan. These old Kurdish principalities still survive in present-day administrative divisions, notably Iran's *ostan* of Kurdistan, formerly Ardalan, with its capital at Sanandaj (earlier known under its Arabic form of Senneh), and Iraq's *liwa* of Sulaymaniya (in Kurdish, Sulaymani; also the name of the capital), which was formerly called Baban after the name of the ruling family.

Fluctuations in the frontier continued into the nineteenth century, when the Western powers, Britain and Russia, intervened to preserve order in this broad buffer zone between their respective Asiatic empires. A four-nation commission surveyed the Ottoman-Iran frontier during 1848-52 and helped to stabilize the southern boundary between Sulaymani and Ardalan-Zohab. Further north, however, ambitious Kurdish chieftains sought to profit from communal conflicts between Kurds and Assyrians; this resulted in the massacre of thousands of Assyrians, the emigration of many more, and the deportation of many Kurds once the Ottoman authorities intervened. The three wars between Turkey and Russia, and to a lesser extent the two between Qajar Iran and Russia, contributed to the continued political fragmentation, demographic upheaval and socioeconomic disorientation of Kurdistan. Christian minorities either fled the war zones to Russian protection or were evacuated (or deported, depending on one's viewpoint) further inland within the Ottoman or Iranian domains. Kurds filled the vacuum, or fought for the Turks, the Iranians or the Russians (who raised two regiments of Kurds during the Crimean War), or against each other, as their interests appeared to dictate. Finally, the vicious circle of Armenian nationalist uprisings and Ottoman reprisals known as the Armenian massacres began in 1894 at Sasun, west of Lake Van, with a bloody clash between Armenians and Kurds.

The Kurds in the Twentieth Century

The dismemberment of Ottoman Turkey after World War I introduced a new phase in this politico-demographic engineering. By the Treaty of Sèvres in 1920, the four northeastern Ottoman vilayets (provinces) were to form an independent Armenia, and a vaguely delineated region stretching south of this area into the vilayet of Mosul was to form an independent Kurdish state. However, following Kemal Atatürk's establishment of the Turkish Republic and his successful fight to preserve the territorial integrity of Anatolian Turkey, the projected independent Armenia was reduced in size and status to the Soviet Armenian Republic and the proposed Kurdistan was rolled back to the vilayet of Mosul. This in turn, by a League of Nations decision in 1925, was awarded to the new Arab kingdom of Iraq under British tutelage. In the same year, Reza Khan overthrew the Qajar dynasty in Iran and, as Reza Shah, embarked on a vigorous policy of centralization and modernization. Since then the three main "hosts" of the Kurds—Iran, Iraq and Turkey—have been able, despite a succession of internal political crises, to maintain their mutual frontiers without overt outside interference and to determine the status and fortunes of a partitioned Kurdistan by fiat from Tehran, Baghdad and Ankara.

Governmental policies have varied widely during the past fifty-five years. Turkey, with the largest Kurdish population and faced with several separatist revolts up until the 1930s, was at first the most uncompromisingly assimilationist. Officially, Kurds did not exist in the Republic from 1934 to 1970; the turbulent inhabitants of eastern Anatolia were referred to as "mountain Turks." From the early 1960s the pressure was eased; articles on the Kurds and Kurdistan were published, bilingual journals appeared, and liberal pressure in the Turkish press and parliament brought official recognition of the right of the Kurds to exist in Turkey. This remains a sensitive frontier, however, and reactions to fighting in the Kurdish areas of Iraq and Iran in recent years have kept the brakes on the practical progress of Kurdish aspirations in Turkey.

In Iran the status of the Kurds has been, superficially, less threatened than in either Turkey or Iraq. The Pahlavi government generally hailed the Kurds as brother Iranians and put few obstacles in the way of Kurdish cultural identity. In practice the Iranian Kurds' closest neighbors, at least in the north, are Shi'i Azerbaijani Turks, and communal distrust is as endemic to Iranian Kurdistan as it is to Turkish and Iraqi Kurdistan. Political challenge, too, has been at least as dramatic. When Reza Shah was forced to abdicate by the Anglo-Russian occupation of 1941, a full-fledged Kurdish separatist organization came into being, with its left wing the stronger of the two, and for eleven months in 1946 an independent state, the Kurdish Republic of Mahabad, enjoyed a precarious existence within the Soviet-sponsored autonomous republic of Azerbaijan that had been proclaimed at Tabriz. This was a "mild, homespun régime, uncertain whether it was independent or autonomous and part of Persia. No one was shot for political reasons and there were two poets on the President's staff."[4] With the withdrawal of the Russians later that year, the Iranian army recovered control of these northwestern provinces and the Mahabad leaders were hanged.

The recent Islamic Revolution in Iran brought renewed separatist hopes and their inevitable suppression by an ideologically different but no less centralizing régime. The referenda on the establishment of an Islamic republic and on its constitution were widely boycotted in the Kurdish areas. During 1979, revolts in Sanandaj, Mahabad and elsewhere were crushed, but guerrilla resistance continues.

The most violent arena of Kurdish separatism has been Iraq. The Kurds of Sulaymani challenged the British mandate in 1919 and again in 1922, after the Treaty of Sèvres had encouraged hopes of independence. Once the Hashemite kingdom of Feisal was securely established in 1930, the government moved to replace Kurdish officials with Arabs and to suppress the teaching of the Kurdish language.

Kurdish woman in traditional attire.

Revolts followed throughout the 1930s and 1940s, in which the Kurds won several spectacular battles but lost the war. The chief guerrilla leader, Mulla Mustafa Barzani, withdrew across the Iranian border in 1945, where his small army supported the Mahabad republic until its fall, then trekked into Soviet territory. The resistance in Iraq went underground, with the formation of the left-leaning Democratic Party of Kurdistan (DPK; also known as the Kurdish/Kurdistan Democratic Party or KDP).

A military coup by 'Abd al-Karim Qasim (Kassem) and the proclamation of an Iraqi republic in 1958 brought high hopes for the realization of Kurdish autonomy. The new constitution hailed the Kurds as partners with the Arabs and guaranteed them full rights within the state; Barzani was welcomed back, Kurdish officials were reappointed, and the KDP came into the open. But practice again failed to keep pace with promises, and a decade of intermittent fighting followed. The Pesh Merga ("those who face death"), as the Kurdish partisans were now known, won more battles and considerable international sympathy, but political divisions among the Kurds and big power strategic aims in the Middle East coincided to nullify these gains. In 1970 the Ba'ath government came to terms: the Kurds were accorded *de jure* as well as *de facto* autonomy and an active role in the central government. A rebellion in 1974 failed and many hard-won political and even cultural concessions were rescinded. Mulla Mustafa Barzani died in 1979, but his son and other leaders continue what must seem even to the sympathetic observer a hopelessly anachronistic struggle in an age when even established nation-states are forfeiting their autonomy to new forms of imperialism.

Social and Cultural Life

Formerly a majority of Kurds were pastoral nomads living in black tents of woven goat hair (as their southern neighbors the Lors to a great extent still do), driving their flocks of sheep and goats up to the hill pastures in spring and down to the valleys in the fall, and practicing seasonal subsistence agriculture. Now they are for the most part sedentary farmers and stockbreeders. Apart from involvement in some processing industries (for example, tobacco at Sulaymani, petroleum at Kirkuk, and textiles and carpets at Sanandaj) the population is still predominantly rural in every host country. Social organization is nevertheless essentially tribal.

The tribe is a recognized device for preserving the history and promoting the solidarity of the Kurds as a whole. Kurdish genealogists and historians, in identifying and relating confederations, tribes, clans, and other subdivisions, take into account territorial contiguity, political and economic association, and feudal allegiance, as well as lineage. The Barzanis, for example, though affiliated with a particular village some fifty miles north of Erbil, originated as a branch of the Naqshbandi Sufi brotherhood before achieving "tribal" status about a century ago. This historical eclecticism is reflected in the Kurdish words for tribal units and leaders, which are etymologically varied: *eshir/ashireh, tā'ifeh* and *khēl* are Arabic, *ēl* Turkish, *tireh* Persian (or at least Iranian) in origin, and chiefs of different sorts may be called *agha* (Turkish), *ra'is* (Arabic) or *pāshā* (Persian).

Kurdish bride (right) with female member of her family.

Men of the Ruwanduz Kurds of northern Iraq.

At the base of this pyramid of tribal organization is the single household, generally a nuclear family, usually monogamous except in the case of the wealthiest men. As in many Middle Eastern societies, marriage among first cousins is common, with a bride price being obligatory as is proof of virginity. Sexual infidelity is punishable by death and divorce by oral repudiation is a husband's prerogative. Electricity, sanitation, health care, and education are still far from universal. Geographical inaccessibility, intermittent warfare, the inevitable civil disabilities suffered by a national minority, combined with tribal convention and Islamic and quasi-Islamic popular practices, make rural Kurdistan an impoverished and backward embarrassment by the standards of the progressive aspirations voiced by most Middle Eastern governments. To even the best-intentioned Iranian, Iraqi or Turkish bureaucrat, "his" piece of Kurdistan is a distant suspect backwater. Yet there is no dearth of trained engineers, doctors and enlightened intellectuals among the militant idealists who form the popular image of the Kurds, and outside observers have been impressed by the priority given to schools, hospitals and economic development under the short-lived autonomous Kurdish administrations at Mahabad in 1946 and Sulaymani in the 1960s and 1970s.

The great majority of the Kurds adhere to Sunni Islam, the majority sect of Islam, and follow the Shafi'i rite. But mountains are traditionally the refuge of heresies. The Yazidis (Yezidis) of northern Iraq, popularly known as "devil worshippers," are just beyond the fringe of Sunni Islam. The Ahl-e Haqq (also loosely termed the "Ali-Ilahi") is a secret syncretistic religion somewhere between an extreme Shi'i sect and a mystical fraternity; their sacred language is Gorani (Gurāni), a non-Kurdish Iranian language spoken west of Kermanshah. (*Gorani* is also widely used to refer to Kurdish peasants of Iraq.) The mainline mystical brotherhoods among the Kurds—a bridge between formal and popular Islam—are the Qadiri dervishes and the Naqshbandi Sufis. At the village level, popular practices that survive from pre-Islamic times—votive pilgrimages to unofficial shrines, conjuration and exorcism of minor spirits, use of talismans and spells for fertility, rainmaking, etc.—are not confined to Kurds, but cut across all ethnic and religious lines in the region.

The old Iranian festival of Noruz, the celebration of the rebirth of the year at the spring equinox, is particularly popular among the Kurds. Other seasonal festivals—lambing, shearing, migration to spring pastures, the loosing

of the rams to the ewes, the harvesting of wheat, barley and mulberries—are all celebrated with songs and dances. Kurdish folk dances vary according to tribe and region, but are predominantly line dances reminiscent of the Balkan *kolo* and *horo* or the Levantine *dabka*. The musical instruments are those common to the Middle East, including the strident *zurna*, a double reed woodwind related to the medieval shawm and modern oboe, and the *tambura*, a small fretted lute used by Ahl-e Haqq devotees to help induce a trancelike state. Folk arts and crafts include jewelry making in silver and semiprecious stones, woodcarving (a specialty of Sanandaj), embroidery, and, of course, carpet weaving.

As a warrior, the Kurd plays *jerid* (marksmanship and tent pegging at full gallop), *chowgan* (polo) and other virtuoso equestrian games common to other Iranian tribes as well as to Turks and Arabs of the region. He is also a keen hunter, fowler, falconer, and fisher in the game-filled hills, and a devotee of chess and backgammon in the teahouses of the towns. If he is literate in Kurdish as well as Persian, Arabic and/or Turkish, he will read and contribute to the poetry, history, political and cultural tracts, and newspapers (some clandestine) that have helped through the last few centuries to consolidate his national identity. If he has studied abroad (and many Kurds today are students in America, Europe and the Soviet Union) he may help to promote his cause in English, French, German, Russian, or Armenian, or add to the vitality of a modern Kurdish literature that draws on world models.

Even if he is illiterate, he—and more especially his mother, father and grandparents—enjoys a rich oral tradition that includes history, legend, poetry, song, folk tale, fable, proverb, and riddle. Much of this is made up of Kurdish variants of recognizable Iranian or general Middle Eastern themes, though Kurdish originality accentuates "the timeless quality of some of the tales, where armoured cars are found disporting themselves alongside the Simurg, where viziers telephone to their kings, and legendary Iranian heroes settle their differences with hand-grenades."[5] Innovation within tradition, whether technical or artistic, poses no paradox for the Kurds; this is undoubtedly one explanation for their survival. ଳ

John R. Perry, associate professor of Persian Language and Civilization at the University of Chicago, has traveled widely in the Middle East, including Kurdish areas.

Notes

1. See Yona Sabar, *The Folk Literature of the Kurdistani Jews* (New Haven and London, 1982), xv, and Margaret Kahn, *Children of the Jinn* (New York, 1980), xi.

2. See Robert Braidwood, "The Agricultural Revolution," *Scientific American* 203, no. 3 (September 1960): 130-48.

3. C. J. Edmonds, *Kurds, Turks and Arabs* (London, 1957), 206f., 246, 332, 368-69.

4. David Adamson, *The Kurdish War* (New York, 1964), 22. For the history of the Mahabad republic, see William Eagleton, Jr., *The Kurdish Republic of 1946* (London, 1963).

5. D. N. MacKenzie, *Kurdish Dialect Studies* (London, 1961–62), vol. 2, xiv. The Simurg[h] is a fabulous bird in the Iranian national epic.

Suggestions For Further Reading

Adamson, David. *The Kurdish War.* New York: Praeger, 1964. A journalist's eyewitness account of the Kurdish struggle in Iraq during the 1960s.

Barth, Fredrik. *Principles of Social Organization in Southern Kurdistan.* Oslo: Brødrene Jørgensen, 1953. Based on field work in Iraq in 1951.

Eagleton, William, Jr. *The Kurdish Republic of 1946.* London and New York: Oxford University Press, 1963. A scholarly and sympathetic account of the short-lived Mahabad republic in Iranian Kurdistan, with much additional general information.

Edmonds, C. J. *Kurds, Turks and Arabs.* London and New York: Oxford University Press, 1957. As well as being a political, diplomatic and military history of the Kurds during Iraq's "birth of a nation" period by one who was in the thick of it, this is a fascinating collection of varied background lore and personal vignettes.

Encyclopaedia of Islam, new ed., s.v. "Kurds, Kurdistān." Compiled by a number of scholars, this article is a comprehensive summary of virtually all aspects of the people, their land, history, and culture. A copious bibliography accompanies every section (there is, however, no mention of rugs).

Hansen, Henny Harald. *Daughters of Allah: Among Moslem Women in Kurdistan.* London: George Allen & Unwin, 1960. A popular account of a Danish ethnographer's field work among Kurdish women in Iraq in the 1950s.

_____. *The Kurdish Woman's Life: Field Research in a Muslim Society, Iraq.* Copenhagen: National Museum, 1961. The scholarly publication of the field work on which the preceding entry is based. Has a section on weaving, including the Kurdish vocabulary.

Kahn, Margaret. *Children of the Jinn.* New York: Wideview Books, 1980. An American student in Azerbaijan learns about Kurds, Turks and Iranians during the Shah's last decade. The sketches of Kurdish women at home are particularly revealing.

Leach, E. R. *Social and Economic Organisation of the Rowanduz Kurds.* London: Percy Lund, Humphries & Co., 1940. Based on 1938 field work in Iraq. Includes some information on looms.

MacKenzie, D. N. *Kurdish Dialect Studies.* 2 vols. London and New York: Oxford University Press, 1961–62. The first volume is a linguistic description of the Iraqi Kurdish dialects; the second is a collection of transcribed texts (conversations, anecdotes and folk tales) with English translations.

Sabar, Yona. *The Folk Literature of the Kurdistani Jews.* New Haven and London: Yale University Press, 1982. Legends, tales, songs, and proverbs from Zakho, in the north of Iraq, with Stith Thompson index and fascinating background notes. Much of the material is too specifically Jewish or too generic Middle Eastern to qualify as strictly Kurdish, but all is entertaining and informative.

Soame, E. B. *To Mesopotamia and Kurdistan in Disguise.* London: John Murray, 1912. Travels in the early twentieth century.

Sykes, M. "The Kurdish Tribes of the Ottoman Empire." *Journal of the Royal Anthropological Institute* 38 (1908): 451-86. Reprinted in: *The Caliphs' Last Heritage.* London: MacMillan and Co., 1915, 553-638. A detailed listing of Kurdish tribes in the early twentieth century.

van Bruinessen, M. M. *Agha, Shaikh and State: On the Social and Political Organization of Kurdistan.* Utrecht: The University of Utrecht, 1978. A dissertation based largely on field work in the 1970s in Kurdish areas of Iran.

The Kurdish Rugs of Iran

Murray L. Eiland

Although Kurds are scattered throughout much of Iran and form one of the country's largest minority groups, their woven products are often misattributed or poorly understood. Clearly they account for many otherwise unidentified rugs from the Hamadan villages, most of the "Bakhtiyari" rugs from the Chahar Mahal, and a number of pieces associated with nomads and villagers from northern Azerbaijan to Varamin, Khorasan and Shiraz. Yet the only rugs consistently labeled as Kurdish—except for those of the Quchan area in northeastern Iran—are those of Senneh (modern Sanandaj), the Bijar area and the numerous villages and diminishing nomadic population of Kurdistan itself. The reasons that Kurds elsewhere are often not identified as the weavers of particular types of rugs are probably related to their flexibility in adapting local styles rather than to any effort to deny them credit. As people who have, in recent times, used rug weaving as a major source of income, the Kurds have become attuned to the needs of the marketplace, and if this involves borrowing styles and designs from their neighbors, then so be it. Some Kurdish rugs from eastern Iran may thus resemble Baluchi rugs, while those marketed in Shiraz show many features of the local Qashqa'i or Khamseh styles.

A collection of Kurdish rugs from Iranian Kurdistan, however, would presumably show something specifically identifiable as Kurdish, and it is an exploration of this issue that I find particularly revealing. Is there something innately Kurdish about these rugs? Can we point to particular designs and designate them as specifically Kurdish? Is there something in the style or use of color that suggests a Kurdish origin? How do we know that a given rug is Kurdish? This discussion should throw some light on these issues.

The Sennehs

Senneh rugs should be the easiest to describe, as they are the product of one city and are so consistent in their structure that they are usually identifiable on that basis alone. They are symmetrically ("Turkish") knotted, with a single weft passing between the rows of knots, and—except for a small minority of especially fine pieces with silk foundation yarns—they are woven on a cotton foundation. Substantially finer in weave than the Hamadan and Chahar Mahal rugs of the same general description, they have alternate warps depressed in a peculiar manner that distinguishes them even from the Malayer, the finest of the Hamadan district weaves. The single wefts are passed under enough tension to depress one warp and push the other forward. This means that one knot will incline in one direction, while the knot in the row below or above will incline in the other. Thus no warp is consistently depressed, and all warps are intermittently raised and depressed from row to row. This gives the rug a particularly rough, grainy feel on the reverse side, and one could virtually identify a Senneh blindfolded.

The origin of weaving in Senneh and the reasons for its peculiar technique are matters of speculation. A. C. Edwards in *The Persian Carpet* suggests that weaving in the Senneh manner began after the town became capital of Kurdistan several hundred years ago.[1] A need was thus created for carpets fine enough to suit the tastes of Persian officials, and this presumably required thin foundation yarns. Perhaps use of a single weft began as a device to make the weave square, with as many knots vertically as horizontally.

The range of designs in Senneh rugs seems surprisingly restricted and virtually every design may be traced to a source outside Kurdistan. More than half of the Senneh rugs I have seen show some form of the Herati pattern, whose origins will be described below. Indeed, this percentage would be even higher in the production of the last several decades and in the flat weaves. Another large group of Senneh rugs has designs of repeating botehs (cat. nos. 1-3), an imported design motif from India. A large percentage of the silk-warped Sennehs show boteh designs, and this may give a clue to the design origin. The silk warps are often found in colored horizontal bands several inches wide, leaving fringes of varying colors. A narrow band of blue may be followed by green and then yellow and red. In the rug trade, these are often called "rainbow warps," and the use of this feature in nineteenth century Senneh rugs is preceded by its use in Moghul rugs of the seventeenth and eighteenth centuries, possibly even earlier. The appearance of an Indian-inspired design with a Moghul technical feature may suggest direct copying of an Indian fabric by the Senneh weavers.

Among the twenty-four Senneh pieces published in the catalogue of the Arthur D. Jenkins collection of flat-woven textiles, thirteen show at least some use of the Herati design, while botehs appear on eight.[2] Yet another piece shows an adaptation of a European floral design, while several others have the kinds of stripes that had become popular in Kashmir textiles of the nineteenth century. Other

Common Senneh botehs (detail of cat. no. 2).

Sennehs show the "Gol Henai" or "Vekilli" designs,[3] both descended from urban floral patterns. Even the medallion format, which is often found with a Herati-covered field, usually shows anchor pendants (cat. no. 4) that identify its source among an earlier generation of Persian urban rugs. For a really unusual Senneh one must search the catalogues of the German specialty houses, where only occasionally something out of the ordinary is encountered.

The two Senneh kilims included here (cat. nos. 6, 8) are atypical in that they employ neither Herati nor boteh designs, although all of the five pile pieces included employ either the boteh or Herati. This is not intended as a criticism, but only as an illustration of the narrow range of design. The rugs themselves illustrate the features that collectors of Sennehs have considered especially desirable. The short pile and fine weave throw the elements of the intricate design into sharp focus, and the exquisitely dyed colors are blended into a subtle tonality that has made the Senneh a much sought-after fabric.

And yet we are hard pressed to identify anything here that is specifically Kurdish.

The Bijars

Unlike Senneh rugs, Bijars are made in more than forty towns and villages in the general area of the small city of Bijar. Like the Senneh rug, the Bijar is symmetrically ("Turkish") knotted and its wefting is also unusual. Not only do we find three weft shots in most Bijar rugs (itself a highly atypical feature in Iran), but they follow two patterns. In some cases there are two thick, taut wefts and one sinuous, thin weft between rows of knots, while in others there are two thin, sinuous wefts and one thick, taut weft. The former technique was widespread throughout Safavid times and it is often described as the technique of the "vase" carpets.

The classic Bijar was woven on a wool foundation and the thick wefts were often cabled with plied yarns twisted together in yet another ply. Use of cotton, for either warp or weft, appears to be a late feature. Of course, the taut wefts cause alternate warps to be depressed and we thus have a thick double-warped carpet. In many of the older Bijars, the wefts were packed in so tightly—with a nail-like rod hit with a hammer according to Edwards—that the resulting fabric had to be rolled rather than folded. This is not so pronounced in contemporary rugs and some of the most recent have a cotton foundation with only two wefts between the rows. Some older rugs that do not seem so compact, particularly when they have only two wefts and incompletely depressed warps, may be variant Kurdish types that do not actually qualify as Bijars. At times, use of the Bijar label can be arbitrary.

The possible structural relationship to Safavid carpets suggests to some that the weaving industry in the Bijar area goes back many centuries, and this may be true. Surely some of the large double-warped rugs with wool foundations, attributed to the early eighteenth or nineteenth centuries, may have been woven in Bijar. Many of these show the harshang design, while a group of large "garden" design rugs have a Bijar-like weave. But there seems to be no way to trace the Bijar to Safavid times.

Clearly the designs are substantially more varied than in Senneh rugs, and it is possible to find Bijar rugs of apparent originality and creativity, although a majority of them, particularly recent production, are woven in the Herati design, while the boteh and Mina Khani design (whose origins are discussed below) make up another large segment. The medallion designs are often relatively simple, with anchor pendants (cat. nos. 11, 15), and production from the turn of the century onward often shows European-style floral devices (cat. no. 13). After we subtract harshang variants (cat. nos. 12, 18), the lattice arabesque (cat. no. 9), and the "weeping willow" (fig. 1),[4] there are few Bijars remaining.

Fig. 1. Rug with "weeping willow" motif along the sides of the main field, collection of Randolph Blake.

18

The classic Bijar, however, has unique characteristics as appealing as those of the Senneh. Here the pile is longer and the wool more lustrous, with colors of great depth and clarity. With a few notable exceptions, the Bijar is not a particularly finely woven rug and yet a curvilinear effect is often achieved with great economy of means. An unusual feature is the appearance of floral devices, particularly in the borders, with no outlines. Late nineteenth century rugs often have wide graceful borders.

The curvilinear effect, of course, requires more concentration from the weaver than many simple geometric patterns, and this appears to have been aided by the use of pattern rugs or vagirehs. These are small pieces (cat. no. 10) in which enough of the pattern is reproduced so that they could serve as a guide for weaving an entire large rug.

There is much conflicting information in the rug trade about a particular group of extremely finely woven Bijars whose knot count may exceed 200 knots per square inch (cat. nos. 13, 14). At times, they have been identified with particular villages or specific workshops. These are even more likely than the most common Bijars (whose knot counts are usually below 100 per square inch) to show classic Persian floral designs, and they are more likely to have cotton foundations. (Note the weave of cat. no. 16.) Such pieces were probably woven from cartoons rather than vagirehs.

The Bijar rugs included here cover an unusually wide range of designs, with two examples of the harshang design. The variety of pieces also shows the range between the curvilinear city-type Bijars (cat. no. 11) and the more geometric village types (cat. no. 18). Until recently, there was apparently a broad spectrum of design sophistication among the villages weaving Bijar rugs, although this seems to have narrowed. Contemporary Bijars are much more finely woven than those of fifty years ago, but they show far less imagination.

Kurdish Village Rugs

While the rugs of Senneh and the Bijar area have established a distinct market identity, those made by the nomads and villagers throughout Kurdistan are usually described under the general label, "Kurdish village rugs" (cat. nos. 22-27). These pieces are of fairly uniform construction, with the symmetrical knot traditionally tied on an all-wool foundation, although more recently some cotton yarns are found. The knotting is rather coarse, alternate warps are at most only slightly depressed, and there are only two wefts between rows of knots. There is nothing remarkable, in my opinion, about the construction of these rugs that would separate them from the rugs of other groups of northwestern Iran. Such diverse peoples as Lors, northern Afshars and Turkic or Persian villagers have woven rugs that are now indistinguishable from the Kurdish village rugs.

In terms of design originality, these rugs present an apparent contradiction. While one could assemble hundreds with significant differences in appearance, a majority are based on the same classic designs as Sennehs and Bijars. At times, the design origins are not immediately obvious, but a great number of rugs show a degenerate Herati (cat. no. 22), Mina Khani or harshang pattern (cat. nos. 21, 23),

while others are filled with simple geometric botehs. Seldom do we see a suggestion of curvilinear design, nor is there the depth and variety of color found in a nineteenth century Bijar.

Nevertheless, there are a number of Kurdish village rugs without obvious links to specific urban types. Many show simple repeating patterns—usually based on stylized floral figures (cat. no. 27)—and field designs with large diamond shapes (cat. nos. 24, 25) and smaller geometric devices (cat. no. 26), while occasionally we see fanciful compositions with human figures and large animal shapes. The more esoteric the designs become, of course, the less certain we may be about their source, since such rugs often show elements suggestive of a Lori or Bakhtiyari origin. The earliest rugs are also the most challenging to date, although I believe pre-1850 Kurdish village rugs are extremely rare.

At the beginning of the twentieth century, runners formed a substantial part of the output from Kurdistan. These were slightly over 3 feet wide and often up to 15 feet long. Often the field was covered with repeating, geometric floral devices. This part of the Kurdish village production seems to have almost disappeared, as the modern Kurdish village rug has become more uniform in size and, like the Sennehs and Bijars, more restricted in design.

It is known that in Persian Kurdistan there are Kurds of the Sanjabi (cat. no. 35), Jaf (cat. no. 40), Kahlor, Qulyahi, Herki, Gurani, and many other tribes, although the term "tribes" may be a misnomer for these largely settled and increasingly heterogeneous groups. I have not traveled widely among the rug-weaving Kurdish villages, but other individuals have come away with the impression that differences in design and rug type are more a matter of local preference than any kind of specific tribal identity. This would be expected from the diverse, external sources of the designs, and yet a search for rugs that may be specific to a particular group uncovers a few suggestions.

The diamond pattern found on several bag faces here (cat. nos. 40, 41) also appears on larger rugs, and the combination of an aberrant technique (most of these pieces show substantial use of offset knotting) and no clearly identifiable outside design source suggests that it may be specific to the Jaf population that has at least woven many examples of it. A related design woven with the offset technique is often found among the Kurds of eastern Turkey and may have a nomadic origin. The flat weaves (cat. nos. 32-34) show geometric figures that—if we had more information—might also point to specific tribal origins, but conclusions in this area would be premature.

The Earliest Kurdish Rugs

Use of the Kurdish label on rugs woven before 1800 is hazardous, although this has not prevented rug scholars from attempting to identify one group or another of early rugs as Kurdish. Perhaps the majority of eighteenth century rugs that are now suspected to be of Kurdish origin are long narrow pieces in the harshang design that may range anywhere from about 5 by 10 feet to upwards of 8 by 24 feet. The width to length ratios may be as small as two to one, but may also exceed three to one. These rugs can be divided into a number of categories based on structure, and related pieces may then be identified.

Fig. 2. Harshang design rug, 85 x
267 inches, probably first half of
the eighteenth century, private collection. Although rugs of this sort
are often labeled as Kurdish, the
asymmetrical jufti knotting here,
along with the colors and wool texture, are more suggestive of an
eastern Persian origin, possibly in
Herat.

Fig. 3. Harshang design rug, 95 x
184 inches, probably from the
Karabagh region, private collection.
Here the harshang is somewhat
stiffer and there has been some design degeneration along the central
axis. Like fig. 2, such rugs are also
often labeled as Kurdish; this example likely dates from the last half of
the eighteenth century.

Possibly the oldest group is exemplified by fig. 2, which shows a particularly early version of the harshang. The large palmettes are still quite elaborate and the central axis of figures has not undergone the series of changes that leads to their simplification.[5] The colors include a surprising prominence of green, with reds based on a cochineal-like dye. The foundation is of hand-spun cotton, with three wefts between the rows of knots and a moderate depression of alternate warps. The surprise, however, is that they are woven with the same variety of asymmetrical jufti knots[6] found in modern Khorasan products such as the "farsibaff" Mashad and Birjand carpets[7] and the wool resembles the soft Khorasan wool found in older Mashad rugs.

Obviously related to these rugs in structure and color is a small group of compartment and tree motif rugs[8] whose origins have long been disputed, as well as a number of less common designs.[9] The compartment and tree rugs have been attributed by Edwards to the Hamadan district village of Famenin,[10] but the recent appearance in the New York trade of a nineteenth century Hamadan-weave version of this design at least suggests that this was a type produced in the Hamadan district rather than the jufti-knotted version. The cochineal-like red, soft wool and Khorasan-type jufti knot all point away from Kurdistan for these rugs, although a number of scholars still support a Kurdish origin.

The next group of oversize harshang rugs—which also includes a number in the related Afshari design—probably does not antedate the eighteenth century (fig. 3). Here the harshang shows some deterioration and the palmettes are not so elaborately drawn. These rugs show no use of cochineal-like reds and the knotting is symmetrical on a wool foundation. But there are aspects of the structure that suggest a close relationship to the Caucasian "dragon" rugs, particularly the appearance every few inches of an especially thick weft made by cabling together a number of other wefts. Perhaps these were intended to mark the rug's progress, as they seem unnecessary for structural purposes, but they relate these pieces to the largest surviving group of "dragon" rugs, which are now often attributed to the Shusha area. Almost certainly this type of large harshang carpet was woven in the Karabagh region.

The next groups of large harshang carpets—and there are hundreds of surviving examples—are symmetrically knotted but otherwise varied technically. They can be divided on the basis of foundation materials. With the cotton foundation examples, whether the design appears close to the original prototype or degenerate, the warps are almost always machine spun, distinguishing them from the jufti-knotted rugs. They are also different in that they have madder reds, little green and in many cases a strong purple. Alternate warps may be flat, depressed or intermediate. Most rug scholars currently label these as Kurdish rugs, but this presents some problems.

If they are Kurdish, where in Kurdistan were they made? They are double wefted and do not in any significant way resemble Sennehs. Similarly, they show different foundation materials and a substantially different texture from Bijars. They are so large that it is hard to imagine that they were woven by nomads or in small villages, and yet there is no clear tradition of such weaving in any Kurdish population center. Even Saujbulagh, a predominantly Kurdish city in Azerbaijan, produces rugs with a wool foundation.

Although the exact origin of these pieces is not clear, I suspect that they were woven in the Heriz district east of Tabriz. It is likely that the medallion design arrived there at about the same time as Western sizes measuring 9 by 12 feet or 10 by 14 feet. What these villages were weaving at an earlier time would probably involve classic patterns such as the harshang. The colors in many of these early rugs, in my opinion, resemble those found in the earliest identifiable Heriz district rugs.

The last group of these early harshang rugs is the most likely to be Kurdish, but it is also puzzling. These rugs are usually not quite so large as the preceding group, but still were woven in a long *kellegi* format.[11] They have wool rather than cotton foundations and they are clearly of the same weave as a number of Mina Khani and Herati pieces. The knotting is coarse and there are usually two wefts between the rows of knots. In color tonality many of these rugs seem similar to the earliest surviving generation of small Kurdish village rugs. Often there is a slight to moderate depression of alternate warps.

These pieces, like the last group, are usually labeled as Kurdish in the rug trade. The question as to whether rugs in these sizes were woven in villages is still open, but surely it is not nomadic work. We must consider the Bijar area as a possible source, although, for the most part, these rugs do not have the triple weft structure found in Bijars. Conceivably this could be a late feature rather than a vestige from an earlier time. Most rugs of this group cannot convincingly be dated any earlier than 1800, which again leaves us with the general question as to the origin of Kurdish weaving and the earliest rugs that can be labeled as Kurdish.

Designs in Kurdish Rugs

Looking at the weaves of Senneh, Bijar and the Kurdish villages of northwestern Iran revealed little that seemed indigenously Kurdish, and it has been difficult to apply the Kurdish label convincingly to any group of rugs dating before the last several centuries. Does a look at Kurds elsewhere alter our perspective?

The Kurds of eastern Turkey weave a substantially different type of rug from that of the Iranian Kurds, but this fact may have a number of explanations. First, the Kurds living within the Ottoman state have been more scattered, they have not had anything like the partial autonomy enjoyed by the Iranian Kurds and apparently little urban tradition has developed among them. While Senneh has been basically a Kurdish city, and Saujbulagh has been a regional Kurdish center, Turkish Kurds have not only been more preponderantly rural, but more nomadic as well. Although hard data to support this view are unavailable, it seems likely that Kurdish ethnic unity in Turkey has been more diffuse, less influential and more isolated from court and urban traditions. Thus it can be noted that Turkish Kurdish rugs follow substantially different traditions having little in common with urban rugs. Whether Turkish Kurdish rug designs are primarily derivative or indigenous must be the subject of a separate investigation.

More relevant is a look at the Quchan Kurds, resettled in Khorasan in 1600 by Shah Abbas, who wished to create a buffer between the villages of Persia and the Turkoman raiders of the north. Elements of the Zafaranlu Kurds were settled around Quchan, while Shadlu Kurds occupied areas around Bojnurd. Tradition maintains that 15,000 families were moved, including Amarlu and Kaiwanlu Kurds. A comparison between weavings of these Quchan Kurds and those of Kurdistan should thus give us a clue as to the state of Kurdish weaving at the time of separation, as there has been little communication since then.

What becomes evident is that at least in pile weaves of the Quchan group, there are rugs with clear borrowing from the Baluchis (many symmetrically knotted Baluchi-appearing rugs are surely of Kurdish weave), from the Turkomans and even from such distant areas as the Caucasus. Although some of the utilitarian flat weaves of the Quchan area resemble those of the Zagros and eastern Turkey, seldom is a Quchan pile rug found that bears any demonstrable relationship to Kurdish rugs from the west.

Several different explanations are possible. It could mean that at the time of separation, there was little or no pile weaving among the Kurds and that the tradition developed subsequently. It could suggest that there are few, if any, surviving tribal designs. It could also be the result of weaving in the two areas developing in divergent directions in response to different markets. It should be noted, for example, that even the Baluchi-inspired rugs are symmetrically knotted and not woven Baluchi style with the asymmetrical knot. This could be interpreted as evidence that the Kurds already had a tradition of weaving pile rugs before they arrived in the east.

A careful analysis of Kurdish rugs from the west, however, provides some possible explanations when considering sources of the designs. While many geometric and stylized designs do not immediately reveal their antecedents, our survey of rugs of the three western Kurdish types —those of Senneh, Bijar and the Kurdish villages—has shown that the overwhelming majority of Kurdish rugs have designs that may be traced directly to a Safavid or Moghul court or urban sources. Furthermore, these designs so common among the western Kurds—and rare in Quchan—had not solidified by the time of the tribal move eastward.

The specific designs I refer to are the Herati, Mina Khani, harshang, and boteh, which are the antecedents of over three-quarters of the western Kurdish rugs woven between 1850 and 1950. Add to this the urban-inspired designs based on an allover arabesque lattice, the medallion and pendants, and less common designs such as the "weeping willow" and the "Gol Henai," and we recognize that it is a rare rug that can even be suspected of showing anything indigenously Kurdish. Much more common are rugs of the late nineteenth and twentieth centuries with a clear borrowing of European floral styles, as in a Bijar published here (cat. no. 13).

I believe the manner in which these designs have evolved is instructive, and the Herati design presents a good example of just how a complex repeating form developed from a group of rug designs that apparently arose within the Moghul court. In its modern form, the Herati design may

Fig. 4. "Indo-Herat" rug, 65 x 153 in., attributed to northern India, seventeenth century, private collection. The palmettes, lancet-shaped leaves and scrolling vinework found in this class of rugs is the source of the Herati design found in so many nineteenth century Iranian rugs.

Fig. 5. Detail of fig. 4. Four lancet leaves are arranged around the lozenge figure formed by the delicate white vinework. At each corner of the lozenge are palmettes. Although this forms only one component in the more complex design of the Indo-Herat rug, it is the combination of motifs repeated in the classic Herati pattern.

be conceived essentially as a lozenge with stylized floral figures at each corner and lancet leaves arranged roughly parallel to the sides of the lozenge. This design can subsequently be repeated throughout the field.

The Herati design appears to derive from a much more elaborate type of design, however, in which the four sides of the lozenge are formed by the intersecting of scrolling vines in a realistically floral format. Prototypes are seen within the large group of seventeenth century rugs often labeled as "Indo-Herats," and here it requires little imagination to pick out the components that solidified during the eighteenth century into the classic Herati (figs. 4, 5).[12]

The harshang also appears to be an Indo-Herat derivative and it echoes the central axis of palmettes in alternate apposition and opposition. The rows of palmettes along the sides alternately point toward the center and the outer border of the rug, while the crablike figure for which the harshang is named seems to derive from a small palmette with four arabesque leaves. The harshang rugs that appear earliest—the jufti-knotted type noted above—have the same red field and bluish green borders found in the Indo-Herats.

Although no examples of the Mina Khani are included here, it is an extremely common design among Kurdish rugs, and it can also be traced convincingly to another group of seventeenth century Persian rugs called "vase" carpets.[13] The arabesque/lattice design (as seen in cat. nos. 9, 10) is also considered to be a late version of a more complex format used in a seventeenth century piece in "vase" carpet style in the Metropolitan Museum of Art known as the Bingham carpet. It has at times been described as Kurdish[14]—probably because of its apparent relationship to a later rug in a similar design from the McMullan collection—but its colors, texture and structure, I believe, are clear indicators of a Kerman origin.

Pear-shaped forms suggestive of the boteh appear in Near Eastern art centuries before the modern era, but the boteh we know on rugs probably goes no further back than the late eighteenth century and there is certainly no trace of it in Safavid carpets. Apparently it is descended from the clusters of leaves and flowers seen on early Kashmir shawls which had an enormous influence upon the textile world.

So if we find that virtually every Iranian Kurdish rug has a design traceable to a foreign source or an earlier urban design, what are we to conclude? Does this justify looking upon the Iranian Kurdish rug as a relatively recent phenomenon, or does what we find in surviving rugs simply represent a modern type of Kurdish rug? Are there any surviving indigenous Kurdish designs in Iranian Kurdistan? Or did the Kurds simply begin weaving rugs for the market—in designs known and appreciated by the market—sometime during the nineteenth century? Surely the predominance of borrowed designs in nineteenth century work explains the apparent break between the western Kurds and those of Quchan, as designs used by the former group had not developed by the time of the separation.

Thus we return to the questions raised at the beginning of this essay—relative to the existence of a specifically Kurdish design tradition—with some observations, if not conclusions. Of course, the available information may be used to support a variety of positions, and admittedly, I have a bias toward seeing the rural rug of the last century as showing, for the most part, urban-derived designs. The rugs selected for inclusion here to a great degree confirm this; we must look long and hard in Iranian Kurdistan for elements that in themselves are specifically Kurdish. Perhaps Kurdish pile rug weaving actually does date back many centuries, yet I believe that there is little trace of a tribal or ethnic tradition surviving in the designs. 🔊

Murray L. Eiland, MD, has written extensively on many aspects of Oriental rugs. His highly acclaimed Oriental Rugs: A Comprehensive Guide *was revised and expanded in 1981.*

Notes

1. A. C. Edwards, *The Persian Carpet* (London, 1953), 121-22.

2. Cathryn Cootner, *Flat-woven Textiles: The Arthur D. Jenkins Collection*, vol. 1 (Washington, D.C., 1981).

3. For the "Gol Henai" design, see Edwards, *The Persian Carpet*, 49-50, fig. 34; for the "Vekilli" design, see ibid., 122 and 128, fig. 120.

4. For the "weeping willow" design (also known as "Bid Majnun"), see ibid., 48, fig. 32 and 131, fig. 125.

5. For a more detailed discussion of this degeneration, see Murray L. Eiland, "The Development of Village and Nomad Rug Designs," *Hali* 4, no. 4 (1982): 338-44.

6. The jufti knot is a double knot, that is, each knot is tied over four warps, resulting in a less densely woven rug.

7. For discussion of the Mashad area rugs, see Edwards, *The Persian Carpet*, 166-69.

8. N. Dimand and J. Mailey, *Oriental Rugs in the Metropolitan Museum of Art* (New York, 1973), 82 and fig. 113.

9. J. Eskenazi, *Il Tappeto Orientale dal XV al XVII Decolo* (Milan, 1982), pls. 28-30.

10. Edwards, *The Persian Carpet*, 92.

11. *Kellegi,* or head piece, is a size of rug, usually 10 to 12 feet long by 5 to 6 feet wide, that is laid across the heads of three other narrow rugs. See Edwards, *The Persian Carpet*, 55f.

12. Murray L. Eiland, *Oriental Rugs: A New Comprehensive Guide* (Boston, 1981), 22f.

13. ibid., 23f.

14. Dimand and Mailey, *Oriental Rugs in the Metropolitan Museum of Art*, 86f., fig. 119 and 113, no. 47.

Kurdish Rugs

𝑛   from

Northeastern

Iran   𝑛

𝑛

Amedeo de Franchis

During past centuries some Kurdish tribes were forcibly resettled by the rulers of Iran in parts of the country hundreds of miles away from their original habitat. Thus, today one finds Kurds in Khorasan, a province that borders the Soviet Union to the north and Afghanistan to the east. History tells us that entire communities of warlike Kurds were sent there in order to create at the eastern frontier a bulwark against recurrent marauding by Central Asian tribes. At the same time the purpose of relieving the insecurity arising from the bloody feuds and divisions of the Kurdish clans in the west was also served.[1]

At the present time Kurdish tribes are established in two areas of Khorasan. The main one lies northwest of the provincial capital, Mashad, and includes the towns of Bajgiran, Bojnurd, Shirvan, Quchan, and Darreh Gaz. The second area is south of Mashad between Nishapur and Sabzavar.[2]

During my stay in Iran from 1970 to 1976, I became particularly interested in the rug production in these areas which, until recently, has maintained a remarkable unity of character. Although the Kurds of Khorasan are not immune to the influence of their Turkoman and Baluchi neighbors, their weavings show very distinctive traits and clearly constitute a separate and coherent group. In many cases, their weavings exhibit a striking similarity to the pieces woven by Kurds in their ancestral homelands in western Iran.

The mention of Kurdish rugs from northeastern Iran is omitted from all of the older books on carpets with the exception of A. C. Edwards' *The Persian Carpet,* which shows one small "Baluch rug woven by Kurds who live in villages north of Meshed."[3]

The scarcity of Western references is due to the fact that the weaving output in Khorasan has always been relatively small, produced mainly for family use rather than for commercial purposes. Few weavings reached the bazaars of Iran, let alone the West. Moreover, it seems that the few pieces that did reach the export market were incorrectly identified and mostly sold in the West as Kazak, Yürük or even Bergama rugs, due to similarities in palette and design with pieces from these origins.

My research is primarily based on data collected during a number of trips made to Khorasan and supplemented by further research in Tehran. In brief, the following descriptions of Kurdish weavings of northeastern Iran are the result of this research.

Pile Rugs

Strong reds, various shades of blue and green, maroon, brick red, ocher, aubergine, and yellow are typical colors. A peculiar shade of copper, fading to tan and possibly due to fuchsin, is found even in the older pieces.

Motifs are strictly geometrical: eight-pointed stars, "Memling" guls (see example in Housego 1978, pl. 138), hooked and stepped lozenges arranged in a vast variety of compositions, often enlarged to form powerful medallions, but sometimes inserted in lattice patterns. Bold colors and stark shapes are successfully combined, providing an impression of basic yet conscious creation, despite some lack of design uniformity.

A typical pattern is the so-called *howzi* ("basin") design, consisting of large rectangular medallions, sometimes crenellated at the sides (fig. 6; for another example see Housego 1978, pl. 137, who refers to it as a "water tank" design). Pointed appendixes depart from the middle of the upper and lower sides of each rectangle and pronged elements are often set vertically on its corners. The medallions may be filled with a great variety of motifs, ranging from large single ones (such as a large eight-pointed star) to tiny repetitive designs. The origin of the *howzi* pattern, which seems to be widespread in the Quchan area, is subject to speculation. The most immediate and obvious interpretation is that it resembles a "garden" pattern.

Other particularly successful designs, which are at their best in older carpets, comprise a type of "scorpion" or "tarantula" motif,[4] recalling patterns in Yürük rugs,[5] and also in Ersari-Beshir pieces.[6] Such a pattern is usually found in a combination of three main colors (light blue, rust red and ocher). It is often associated with a border stripe of reciprocal crosses in blue and blackish brown.

Another interesting pattern is a repeat of ascending multicolored calyx shapes enclosing a small flower. In more recent pieces such a layout appears frozen into a small lattice pattern.[7]

Fig. 6. Kurdish Pile Rug, northeastern Iran, collection of Amedeo de Franchis.

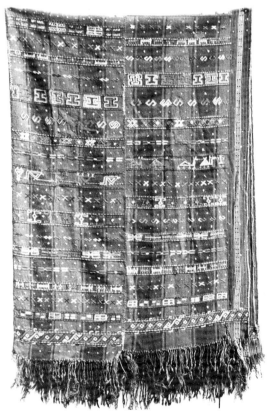

The influence of the Turkoman environment can predominate in some carpets featuring guls or other characteristic motifs.[8] Though not substantially different in structure from the types described above, these particular rugs are, from the point of view of design, a hybrid class. The patterns of several Turkoman tribes can be recognized in unfamiliar shades of light green, vermillion, sky blue, and yellow, intermingled with typically Kurdish motifs. The scale and proportions of the composition are usually different from those of the original Turkoman model and the overall effect is intriguing, but not displeasing, if judged without preconceived standards.

Border patterns are usually narrow, the main border usually having stark geometrical designs on an ivory ground. A particular class of antique, brightly colored carpets in soft deep wool has a bold red and white trefoil design in the border. Of the secondary borders—many of which clearly show Turkoman influence—the most common is a succession of quartered squares skewered by a continuous line as in fig. 6. Also typical is a narrow serpentine pattern composed of light blue, rust red and white segments. Sizes of Khorasani rugs vary. Antique specimens tend to be long and rather narrow but squarer pieces of medium size are also found; runners are very rare. The pile is often long and soft and the handle of the rugs can be thick and "meaty" as in old Kazaks.

Flat-woven Covers

It has been noted that certain weaving techniques suggest particular patterns to the traditional weaver.[9] This also seems to be the rule for the Kurds of Khorasan since the patterns in their pile carpets are markedly distinct from those of their flat-woven rugs and covers.

Pieces in weft float brocading and in extra-weft wrapping usually show a succession of horizontal stripes with motifs that probably constitute the oldest pattern concept in rug weaving (fig. 7). An almost complete spectrum is spanned from basic unornamented band types to complex specimens where the entire fabric is patterned in multiple colors by different woven structures (fig. 8). Often, but by no means always, the more elaborate pieces show a tendency to a more finite layout, mainly by being surrounded

Fig. 7. Kurdish Kilim, northeastern Iran, collection of Amedeo de Franchis.

Fig. 8. Kurdish Jajim (detail), northeastern Iran, collection of Parviz and Manijeh Tanavoli.

by borders, while the simpler ones normally do not. Quality in these pieces is, therefore, a function of the successful combination of various factors: weave, pattern, design, and color.

It is a matter of pride to a weaver when no design stripe in the field is repeated. But often a well-balanced repetition of linear designs or the alternation between decorated bands and those in plain weave can provide a particular rhythm to a piece, pleasing the eye. Such specimens follow the typical Islamic format of an endless repeat.

Motifs are purely geometrical, the diamond reigning supreme in all its possible latch-hooked variations. Sometimes the central stripe is the widest and has designs larger in scale. Not unusual is an allover grid pattern in multiple vivid hues resulting in a bold and aggressive effect (cat. no. 37), as in a medieval banner. Turkoman motifs also occur, probably borrowed from neighboring Yomuts and other tribes. Sometimes, even small animals are included in starkly geometric renditions.

Main borders are normally a succession of ornamented diamonds or other geometric figures while secondary bands contain variations of the "running dog" motif or, more strikingly, a reciprocal horned design in old Turkish tradition commonly found in Turkoman, Baluchi and East Turkestan carpets.[10]

There are times when the borders on the ends are different from those on the sides and when they vary continuously, these different designs succeeding one another in a seemingly random fashion add a wild and spontaneous charm to the piece. Some examples also have large, brilliantly decorated skirts at the ends.

Colors are deep. Rust red often predominates, followed by several hues of blue. Green and yellow add finesse while white provides touches of light. Here also, as in many other rugs of village and nomadic origin, the impression is that older pieces tend on the whole to be brighter and to contain a greater variety of shades. Modern examples usually include orange and purple. While on a visit to Quchan in 1972, I observed a piece with luminous synthetic yarns! Traditional examples would be made entirely of wool, with only occasionally some white cotton added for contrast.

Kilims in slit or dovetailed tapestry seem to be uncommon in Kurdish Khorasan. The only piece I have encountered in slit tapestry is a very finely woven animal cover with two hexagonal medallions on a diaper-patterned background of tiny insectlike motifs.

Large antique textiles of elongated shape and rather limp handle showing multicolored designs on a background of dark blue with longitudinal border bands in rust brown are occasionally found. Examples of similar dimensions and color scheme have been observed in use by Kurds in other areas, and so it can be surmised that these pieces were intended to be dividing curtains for large tents belonging to chieftains.[11] The designs are often striking: flowers, animals and even accurately drawn men and women in local attire indicating the importance these pieces had in the traditional tribal household.

Containers of Various Kinds

Sacks and bags are mostly flat-woven (figs. 10-14) or in alternating pile and flat-woven bands. Pieces entirely in pile are relatively scarce. Flat-woven bags are similar in structure and design to the coverings described above but the quantity of pieces made in slit tapestry weave is significantly higher (cat. no. 36), especially in smaller sizes. Sometimes it is difficult to distinguish pieces in extra-weft wrapping from those made by Kurds in western Iran or Turkey, but the weave is generally finer and the colors softer. Secondary and border motifs are mostly different; examples from Khorasan often bear a trace of Central Asian influence.

The abundantly produced small flat-woven cushions and pillows are particularly fine in weave and design.

Sofrehs

*Sofreh*s are spreads originally associated with traditional bread making and meals. Their ritual significances, which seem to be multiple and profound, have yet to be fully clarified.[12] In more recent times, the Kurds of Khorasan have been major producers of the more typical elongated *sofreh*s which were also distributed elsewhere within Iran. Particularly long pieces are known as "bridal paths," implying a relationship between the *sofreh* and the wedding ceremony which in Iran is centered on a symbolic meal.[13]

The Khorasan Kurdish *sofreh* (fig. 9) generally has a plain central panel in camel-colored wool framed by a decorated border. Long and narrow black triangles ("teeth") based on the lateral borders jut into the central field. They are known in the local vernacular as "fingers" or "nails." The central panel is either empty or decorated with a pole of rather startling motifs . A Kurdish *sofreh* with pile borders is rarely found and then it is probably a consequence of Baluchi influence, which can also result in a squarer shape.

Further study is warranted on the Kurdish tribal weavings from Khorasan in order to pinpoint with greater precision the various origins and cross influences that have contributed to the development of such a distinctive weaving type.

An interesting issue is whether or not the features that differentiate the rugs of the Khorasani Kurds from those woven by their neighbors are due to an ancestral tradition dating from before their removal to eastern Iran. While the striking similarities with weavings produced hundreds of miles to the west (for example, compare fig. 10 with cat. nos. 32 and 62) would seem to point to an affirmative answer, further comparative analysis and research would be needed to set the case on firmer ground. ☸

Amedeo de Franchis is an Italian diplomat whose lengthy residence in Iran gave him the opportunity to study firsthand the weavings of that country's various ethnic groups. He has published a number of articles on Iranian weavings.

Fig. 9. Kurdish Sofreh, northeastern Iran, collection of Amedeo de Franchis.

Notes

1. For the Kurdish emigration to northeastern Iran, see M. M. van Bruinessen, *Agha, Shaikh and State: On the Social and Political Organization of Kurdistan* (Utrecht, 1978), 215-20.

2. See the Iranian publication *Iran Almanac,* 1971 edition, 568, which lists the Kurdish tribes in Khorasan as follows: Shadlu, Zafaranlu, Ghovanlu, Amarlu, Tupkallu, totaling about 100,000 families.

3. A. C. Edwards, *The Persian Carpet* (London, 1953), 192, fig. 179.

4. See Jenny Housego, *Tribal Rugs* (London, 1978), pl. 81.

5. A Yürük carpet in a related pattern is pictured in U. Schürmann, *Oriental Carpets* (London, 1968), 26.

6. For an Ersari carpet in a very similar pattern, see U. Schürmann, *Central-Asian Rugs* (Frankfurt, 1969), pl. 43. For a discussion of this pattern in Ersari weavings, see H. Bidder, *Carpets from Eastern Turkestan* (New York, 1964), 79.

7. For an example, see A. R. de Leon, *Guide en couleurs du tapis* (Paris, 1967), 155.

8. See R. Gardiner, *Oriental Rugs from Canadian Collections* (Toronto, 1975), pls. 62-63.

9. See A. de Franchis and J. Wertime, *Lori and Bakhtiyari Flatweaves* (Tehran, 1976), 22-23.

10. For a point of view on the origin of this motif, see H. Bidder, *Carpets from Eastern Turkestan,* 67.

11. I am indebted to Dr. Peter Andrews for pointing this out to me during the 1983 International Conference on Oriental Carpets in London.

12. See Gerd Näf, "Sofreh and Ru-Korssi," *Hali* 5, no. 2 (1982): 125f.

13. For one such "bridal path," see Jay and Sumi Gluck, *A Survey of Persian Handicrafts* (Tehran, 1977), 315.

Fig. 10. Kurdish Saddle Bag, northeastern Iran, 52 x 25 in., collection of Glenna and Robert Fitzgerald.

The Principal Types 𝓃

𝓃 **and Woven Structures of**

Kurdish Weavings in

𝓃 **Northeastern Iran**

𝓃

John T. Wertime

Fig. 11. Kurdish Saddle Bag, north-
eastern Iran, 52 x 24 in., Trocadero
Oriental Rug and Textile Art,
Washington, D.C.

The nomadic pastoralists and villagers of the Near East and Central Asia have traditionally satisfied many of the requirements of their material and spiritual existence by means of the textiles they produce. While basic needs differ little from group to group, the choice of both woven types and woven structures has varied considerably.

Several factors have influenced the types of weavings produced by these groups of nomads and villagers. Among these are the type of shelter utilized and the mode of transportation employed, especially the kind of pack animals used. A third factor, custom, can also be cited. Initially, however, weaving preference must have been based on the need for shelter, transportation or other necessities of life.

Since weavings are produced for use in conjunction with a particular type of dwelling, it is not surprising that there should be a variety of types and formats in both the pile and flat-woven textiles found in the heartland of the Oriental rug world. Examples of housing include the rectangular black goat hair tents (in which the poles and covering are interdependent), the traditional dwelling of the Kurds of the Quchan-Bojnurd region; the round trellis tent (in which the frame, once erected, is capable of standing on its own without any support from the felt covering), the sort of tent utilized by the Kurds' nearby neighbors, the Turkomans; and the mud brick and other types of permanent houses in which villagers normally dwell. The trellis tent, for example, has requirements as well as possibilities for woven types that in certain cases diverge significantly from those of the black tent or the permanent edifice. Furthermore, the interior space and the way it is utilized are not the same in each.

Transportation of goods and people by means of animals dictates woven types different from those intended for use on a wheeled conveyance. The animals themselves vary in size and shape, and woven containers made to be hauled by them reflect this. For example, very large saddle bags of the kind used by the Lors and Bakhtiyaris of western Iran on donkeys, mules and cattle are awkward on a camel and do not form part of the weaving repertoire of the neighboring Qashqa'is for whom the camel is a common beast of burden. Animal covers and trappings are necessarily made with specific kinds of animals in mind.

Where there are differences in shelter and modes of transport, there are plausible reasons for variations in woven types. When such differences do not exist or are not relevant, what explanations can be found? Why, for example, do the Kurds of the Quchan-Bojnurd region use salt bags with a narrow neck and wider body, whereas the nearby Turkomans use a rectangular bag for salt? Why are shaped salt bags not found to any significant extent, if at all, among Kurdish weavings from Turkey? Did the Kurds of Khorasan bring the tradition of that type of bag with them from the west, or acquire it from neighboring peoples in northeastern Iran? Unfortunately, given the present state of our knowledge, the best we can do is to attribute such variations to tribal or local custom or preference.

The distribution of woven structures is another matter that does not lend itself to easy answers. Is the occurrence of woven structures related in any way to ethnic groups? Does a particular type of dwelling (for example, the trellis tent) imply use of a particular woven structure? Most likely the answer is no, but these and other questions need to be considered.

The question can be raised of whether there is an economic basis for the use of pile versus flat-woven fabrics. Does utilization of one or the other indicate greater or lesser wealth? Certainly pile weavings require more material and time to make than most flat weaves. Is the relative dearth of pile weavings in a group a sign of economic weakness or an indication of some other factor? Why was one flat-woven structure used instead of another?

The nomadic pastoralist and village-based weaver's repertoire of woven types and structures has probably undergone fewer changes than any other aspect of the textile art. This, together with the fact that they can be readily described, makes them good places to begin an attempt to define the essential characteristics of a weaving tradition. In time, we should strive for a clear picture of the types of weavings and fabric structures produced by the different Kurdish groups of the Near East. When this has been achieved, answers to some of the questions raised above will perhaps be found more easily. What follows is a brief attempt to describe the woven types[1] and structures[2] utilized by the Kurds of northeastern Iran.

Bags and Containers

Saddle Bags
Saddle bags are among the most commonly encountered weavings of the Kurds of northeastern Iran. Normally these bags are not much larger than 4 by 2 feet, with very small ones appearing only occasionally. In many examples a panel connects the two pouches. This panel is often fairly wide (6 inches or more) and can be elaborately patterned in a variety of structures. Closure panels of slits and loops are lacking in many examples. Back halves in these and the other types of bags described below are normally woven in weft-faced plain weave. Some are completely plain, while others have narrow multicolored stripes or extra-weft patterning in varying degrees. On the front half of any saddle bag one of the following six structural features usually predominates:

1. Extra-weft wrapping that patterns a plain-weave ground all over (one ground weft after each wrapping weft): 3-movement 2/4 reverse horizontal with the 2-span floats alternately and/or vertically aligned (fig. 10; a very similar piece is published in Housego 1978, pl. 135).

2. Extra-weft wrapping that patterns a plain-weave ground all over (one or two ground wefts after each wrapping weft): 3/2 (2/1) diagonal with the oblique spans usually on the front. This and the above are the most common structures in saddle bags.

3. Slit tapestry weave with outlining in diagonal and horizontal extra-weft wrapping. Some eccentric wefting occurs.

4. Balanced or warp-predominant plain weave patterned in certain areas by extra-weft wrapping: horizontal (2/4 reverse, etc.), diagonal (2/3 reverse, etc.), vertical (2/2). Stars or rosettes are the most common patterns.

5. Extra-weft cut pile wrapping patterning a plain-weave ground all over: Bu1Fo2Bu1 (symmetrical pile segment or "symmetrical knot" in traditional terminology), 2 ground wefts after each row of pile wefts.

6. Weft-faced plain weave patterned in lateral bands by extra-weft cut pile wrapping: Bu1Fo2Bu1; in some examples where diagonal lines are needed, pile segments with a movement sequence and numerical order of Bu2Fo3Bu1 appear. Pile and flat-woven bands alternate in these bags (fig. 11).

Large Sacks

Large sacks are relatively numerous. Normally they are longer than they are wide (measuring approximately 3½ by 2½ feet in some larger pieces), though some tend to be almost square. In a majority of examples the patterning consists primarily of 3/2 (2/1) diagonal extra-weft wrapping (3-movement 2/4 reverse horizontal extra-weft wrapping occurs much less frequently in these than in saddle bags). The diagonally oriented extra-weft wrapping either completely covers the plain-weave ground on the entire front half of the sack or covers the ground weave in wide lateral bands only, the rest of the front half consisting of unpatterned weft-faced stripes and/or weft-faced plain-weave bands patterned by extra-weft wrapping in certain areas only (fig. 12). In other large sacks the primary structure is weft float brocading with weft floats of variable length alternating on the two faces of a weft-faced plain-weave ground. Slit tapestry weave only occasionally forms the predominant structure of these bags.

Pillows and Cushions

The pillows and cushions woven in some numbers by the Kurds of northeastern Iran are much greater in length than in width. Many measure from 2½ feet to a little over 3 feet long and are seldom more than a few inches over a foot wide. Very frequently the principal structure of the front half is slit tapestry weave. Outlining by means of wrapping wefts is common, as is a certain amount of eccentric wefting. The forms of extra-weft wrapping described above in discussing saddle bags (figs. 10,11) constitute the predominant structures in some pillows and cushions. Front halves in pile composed of symmetrical segments (Bu1Fo2Bu1) are also found.

Salt Bags

Like the typical salt bag[3] made in other parts of Iran as well as in Afghanistan, Pakistan and the Transcaucasus, those of northeastern Iran have a narrow neck and wider body. As the principal structure, most of them feature 3/2 (2/1) diagonal extra-weft wrapping that patterns a plain-weave ground all over. Other predominant structures include extra-weft cut pile wrapping (Bu1Fo2Bu1), 3-movement 2/4 reverse horizontal extra-weft wrapping, and balanced plain weave patterned by horizontal, vertical and diagonal extra-weft wrapping (fig. 13).

Miscellaneous Small Single Bags

Small single bags from the Quchan-Bojnurd area are rarely seen. The few examples that can be attributed to that region are woven primarily in 3/2 diagonal extra-weft wrapping (fig. 14).

Fig. 12. Kurdish Sack, northeastern Iran, 41 x 30 in., collection of Glenna and Robert Fitzgerald.

Coverings, Cloths and Spreads

Pile Rugs

The extra-weft cut pile wrapping that forms the pile of the Kurdish rugs of Khorasan (fig. 6) is of the symmetrical type (Bu1Fo2Bu1). The ground weave of these rugs varies from piece to piece. Some rugs have as few as two interlacing ground wefts after each row of pile segments, while in others as many as eight can be found. In most, however, the range is three or four. Usually these wefts are wool and are rather consistently dyed some shade of red (or reddish brown). Warps normally lie on one level. The number of pile segments per square inch is usually low, in many rugs around fifty. Generally, an area of weft-faced plain weave several inches in length is found at both ends. This is often a plain red, though stripes also occur. One or more rows of 2-color 2-strand weft twining appear in the ends of many examples. The edges most often consist of two to four bundles of two warps each, and are attached by means of interlacing ground wefts, sometimes with supplementary wefts added.

Kilims

Khorasani Kurdish kilims are generally thick and heavy and contain several different fabric structures. Almost all are woven in one piece and normally range from about 9 to 13 feet in length and about 4½ to 6½ feet in width.

The format of a majority of these textiles is based on lateral bands which, quite often, have only a partially patterned weft-faced plain-weave ground. The structures used for this patterning are usually weft float brocading with weft floats of variable length alternating on the two faces of the fabric (fig. 7) or extra-weft wrapping. Various forms of extra-weft wrapping also pattern the ground weave all over in individual bands. Less common, but not unusual, are kilims in which different varieties of extra-weft wrapping pattern the ground weave all over most of the textile (cat. no. 37). A rare example woven in dovetailed tapestry weave provides a significant exception to the norm.

Whatever the structural composition of the interior field, these kilims are almost invariably surrounded by borders in extra-weft wrapping and have red weft-faced plain-weave skirts at either end. The skirts may be patterned by small motifs in various structures and/or several rows of 2-color 2-strand weft twining.

Cloths and Spreads (Sofreh)

Kurdish sofrehs[4] are typically flat-woven with areas of pile only occasionally occurring in the center of the field. Most measure 5 to 8 feet in length and 2 to 3 feet in width. A standard feature is the weft-faced plain-weave ground with long, narrow "teeth" in slit tapestry weave projecting inward from the borders on either side. Usually these "teeth" are outlined by 2-color 2-strand weft twining and are patterned by various motifs in extra-weft wrapping. In many examples the field shows no other patterning, with the occasional exception of a small lozenge.

There is, however, a more elaborately decorated type of sofreh in which the central field is patterned by one or more vertically oriented poles (fig. 9; see also Housego 1978, pl. 134). Structures that play a prominent role here are as follows: weft float brocading with weft floats of variable length forming diagonal and/or vertical lines on the front of the fabric and with the pattern wefts carried diagonally and/or vertically on the back to the next shed; weft float brocading with weft floats of variable length alternating on the two faces of the fabric; and extra-weft wrapping: 3/2 (2/1) diagonal, 2/2 vertical, 3-movement 2/4 reverse horizontal, and 2/4 reverse horizontal. The borders surrounding this interior are most often woven primarily in extra-weft wrapping (especially 3/2 [2/1] diagonal) which patterns the ground weave all over; 2-color 2-strand weft twining appears commonly in the upper and lower borders. Weft-faced plain-weave skirts are found at both ends.

Covers and Wrappers (Jajim)
The standard type of *jajim*[5] is made up of narrow widths of warp-faced plain weave that is patterned by warp substitution in regularly spaced vertical bands. These widths, which measure 14 to 15 inches in one example and 22 to 23 inches in another, are sewn together along their selvedges to form rectangular or squarish textiles that often measure up to 7 or more feet in length and 6 or more feet in width. In a few rare examples narrow pile borders appear at both ends and tufts of silk and cotton are inserted in horizontal rows (fig. 15).

Another type of *jajim* made by the Khorasani Kurds consists of fairly wide widths of balanced to warp-predominant plain weave patterned in certain areas by different forms of extra-weft wrapping and 2-color 2-strand weft twining (fig. 8). In both types of *jajims*, variation in the color of the warps produces vertical stripes.

Animal Accouterments

Animal Covers
Animal covers are normally rectangular or squarish (fig. 16). Few, if any, have breast flaps or are shaped in any special way. Dimensions range on the average from 5 to 6 feet in length and from 4 to 5 feet in width. Most are woven in two pieces and sewn together along their selvedges. In a majority of examples the upper third to half consists primarily of stripes in weft-faced plain weave, which may or may not be patterned by extra-weft wrapping, weft substitution, or some other structure. The lower two-thirds or half is much more elaborate, with a complete set of borders enclosing a field of horizontal bands. Extra-weft wrapping (3/2 diagonal, 2/2 vertical and 4/2 horizontal) is the predominant structure here, patterning the plain-weave ground all over in the borders and in many of the lateral bands. Bands of partially patterned or unpatterned weft-faced plain weave also occur in varying frequency in this area. At the bottom of the cover there is usually a skirt of weft-faced plain weave featuring a row of tufts made up of symmetrical (Bu1Fo2Bu1) pile segments. In one example examined, these tufts were asymmetrical, open to the left (Fu1o1Bu1). Long tassels are often found at the lower end. They are composed of bundles of unutilized warps around which multicolored yarns are wrapped and to which tufts of yarn are tied at the end.

What may be another type of animal cover also consists of two rectangular widths sewn together, but is somewhat smaller (one example measures 4 feet 4 inches by 3 feet 7 inches) than the usual variety and is woven entirely in slit tapestry weave except for the weft-faced plain-weave skirts at both ends.

Saddle Covers
Saddle covers are rarely encountered. One example measures 2½ by 2½ feet, has a slit for the saddle horn, and is woven in extra-weft cut pile wrapping with asymmetrical segments open to the left (Fu1o1Bu1). The warp is black goat hair and consists of two Z spun single yarns plied together in the S direction (Z 2 S).

Tent Furnishings and Clothing

Dividing Curtains
Large textiles probably intended for use in chieftains' tents as dividing curtains[6] have been produced by the Kurds of Khorasan. They are woven in two pieces and sewn together along their selvedges, creating, in one example, dimensions of 13 feet 3 inches in length and 5 feet 8 inches in width. Structurally, these rare weavings have a balanced to warp-predominant plain-weave ground that is patterned in certain areas by extra-weft wrapping (horizontal, diagonal, vertical, and reverse horizontal with the spans vertically aligned). The wrapping wefts are spaced, a feature hardly ever seen in the other flat weaves of this group. Since these curtains were meant to be hung horizontally, the axis of the patterns is perpendicular to the warps.

Puttees
Puttees[7] for men are woven in very fine warp-faced plain weave and are patterned at one end in silk principally by diagonal extra-weft wrapping, with some horizontally and vertically oriented wrapping; 2-color 2-strand weft twining is also commonly used. Tufts of symmetrical pile segments (Bu1Fo2Bu1) appear in these textiles, which usually measure approximately 2½ by 6 feet.

The warps and wefts of the Kurdish weavings of the Quchan-Bojnurd area almost invariably consist of two Z spun single yarns that have been plied in the S direction (Z 2 S). The material of the warps is most often undyed ivory wool, though light to dark brown wool does appear. Wefts are normally wool dyed some shade of red (or reddish brown). Warps and wefts of goat hair are not uncommon.

Most flat weaves of northeastern Iran are multistructural, with three or more woven structures appearing in many examples. Recurrent secondary structural features not mentioned above include the following: weft float brocading with the extra wefts interlacing 2/2 on a plain-weave ground and the 2-span floats alternately or vertically aligned and entirely covering the ground weave; extra-weft wrapping on a plain-weave ground with two wefts of different color moving Bo2Fu2o2u6 to create alternating pairs of 2-span floats; and brocading on a plain-weave ground with a single extra weft interlacing two or three warp units (of 2 warps each) 1/1. ⁊

John T. Wertime resided in Iran for a number of years. He became interested in the technical aspects of weavings and has pioneered an innovative system for describing their structures.

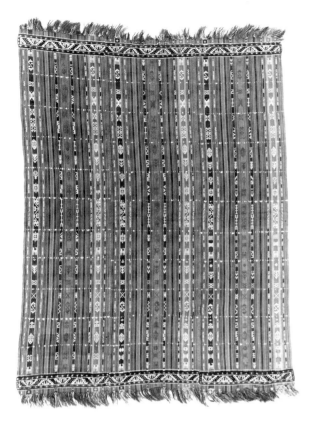

Notes

1. For a description of most of the woven types mentioned below, see John T. Wertime, "The Names, Types, and Functions of Nomadic Weaving in Iran," in Landreau, ed., *Yörük: The Nomadic Weaving Tradition of the Middle East* (Pittsburgh, 1978), 23-26.

2. The discussion of fabric structures in this paper is based on the following articles: Wertime, "Flat-woven Structures Found in Nomadic and Village Weavings from the Near East and Central Asia," *Textile Museum Journal* 18 (1979): 33-54; idem, "Weft-wrapping in Nomadic and Village Flat-woven Textiles from the Near East and Central Asia," in Cootner, ed., *Flat-woven Textiles: The Arthur D. Jenkins Collection*, vol. 1 (Washington, D.C., 1981), 175-91; idem, "A Brief Introduction to the Woven Structures Found in the Jenkins Collection," ibid., 193-99; idem, "A Checklist of Flat-woven Structures Found in Village and Nomadic Weavings from the Near East and Central Asia," ibid., 200-203; idem, "A Note on Describing the Structures of Woven Fabrics Patterned by Supplementary Wefts," ibid., 203; idem, "A New Approach to the Structural Analysis of the Pile Rug," *Oriental Rug Review*, June 1983, 12-16.

3. See John T. Wertime, "Salt Bags from Iran," *Hali* 2, no. 3 (1979): 198-205. I now believe that the bag shown on page 203 is from the Transcaucasus or northwestern Iran rather than being a Kurdish piece from Khorasan.

4. See Gerd Näf, "Sofreh and Ru-Korssi," *Hali* 5, no. 2 (1982): 125f.

5. See John T. Wertime, "Jajims," *Oriental Rug Auction Review*, November 1981, 15f. (also the errata in the December 1981 issue, 29).

6. The particular use of the large textiles described in this section was suggested by Dr. Peter Andrews during the 1983 International Conference on Oriental Carpets in London. In a subsequent personal communication, Dr. Andrews, who has done extensive field work on tents in Iran and Turkey, indicated that the only groups in this region in which he has encountered elaborate dividing curtains have been Kurdish. He says that dividing curtains with stripes in the warp direction and patterned bands in the weft direction are typical of Arab weavings in Arabia. He is therefore inclined to attribute such textiles to Arab influence in the ruling families of certain Kurdish tribes, as indicated by M. Sykes, "The Kurdish Tribes of the Ottoman Empire," *Journal of the Royal Anthropological Institute* 38 (1908): 451-86, reprinted in M. Sykes, *The Caliphs' Last Heritage* (London, 1915): 553-638.

7. See Iran Ala Firouz, "Needlework," in Gluck and Gluck, eds., *A Survey of Persian Handicrafts* (Tehran, 1977): 241. The figures on the lower left and lower right are entirely woven, whereas those above them are embroidered.

Fig. 15. Kurdish Jajim (with pile borders at the ends), northeastern Iran, 85 x 64 in., collection of Edgar and Joy Bulluck.

Fig. 16. Kurdish Animal Cover, northeastern Iran, 60 x 52 in., collection of Amedeo de Franchis.

The

ℛ Weavings of

Iraqi Kurdistan

ℛ

ℛ

William Eagleton

The Kurdish weavings of Iraq, compared to those of Turkey and Iran, are relatively unknown to experts, collectors and dealers. This was not always the case. At the beginning of the twentieth century, John Kimberly Mumford and Walter Hawley presented their studies to the American public in books both entitled *Oriental Rugs*.[1] Both spoke of "Mosul fabrics," although Mumford caused some confusion by placing them within his Caucasian classification. These early descriptions fit nearly all of the Kurdish rugs now woven in Iraq as well as some from north of the border in Kurdish areas of Turkey. Even in Mumford's time, the Mosul label had become a catchall term for rugs of many origins that were collected in northern Iraq, then part of the Ottoman Empire, and sold in the city of Mosul across the Tigris from the ruins of ancient Nineveh.[2] By the end of World War I, Mosul was no longer a collection point, but the Mosul label shifted to Iran to describe low quality Kurdish rugs woven in the Hamadan-Zenjan district. Murray Eiland, in his book *Oriental Rugs: A Comprehensive Guide*, has quite reasonably suggested that the term "Mosul" be dropped altogether, since it has lost whatever meaning it might once have had.[3]

The Kurds of Iraq

The Kurds of Iraq have been separated from those further north only since the early 1920s when the frontier between an independent Iraq and the new Republic of Turkey was delineated. At that time, this new state, with a population approximately eighty percent Arab and twenty percent Kurdish, entered the history of the Middle East. In the 1980s, the numerical size of Iraq's 2.8 million Kurds does not match the estimated Kurdish populations of Turkey or Iran. Nevertheless, the percentage of Kurds in Iraq is the highest of all three and this fact has given them a special place in modern Iraqi and Kurdish history. This is not the place to recount the sixty-year saga of Kurdish revolts and wars against, and reconciliations with, central governments. Suffice it to say that Kurdish pressures, along with accommodations by Baghdad, have gained for the Kurds of Iraq a greater measure of cultural freedom than elsewhere; here, the Kurdish language, dress, music, and traditions all flourish.

Most of the Kurds of Iraq were until recently organized along tribal lines. This is true of Turkey and Iran as well, but in those two countries the ethnic dividing line between

Kurds and non-Kurds has been less clear than in Iraq. Along the fringes of Iranian Kurdistan a nontribal or mixed population has existed for many years in villages that were sometimes under the feudal influences of local khans or princes.

Although many nontribal Kurds can be found in Kirkuk, Erbil, Sulaimaniya, Ruwanduz, and in rural areas as well, most Iraqi Kurds are associated by tradition, if not current loyalty, with one or another of the hundred or so Kurdish tribes of Iraq. The term "shaikh," which is used by Arabs for tribal leaders, is a religious title for the Kurds. So is the title "sayyid," which indicates descent from the Prophet Muhammad. The shaikh and his followers occupy an area and exert influence similar to that of a tribe, and their religious authority may extend beyond a single tribe. In its simplest form, all members of the tribe claim common ancestry; the tribal chiefs, usually called aghas, are the leaders of the most powerful sections. In some tribes, the chiefs have at times in the past come from outside to seize authority and form a separate nobility. These chiefs may be called either aghas or begs, and their relationship to the tribesmen is usually more feudal than tribal. There are enough combinations of these basic types to render generalizations misleading.

The vast majority of rural Kurds live the entire year in their small villages where they keep cattle, sheep, goats, and fowl and cultivate the rain-fed land. Until recently, about five percent of Iraqi Kurds were fully nomadic. These included the great Herki tribe in the north and sections of the Jaf tribe in the south. Both tribes were, and to some extent still are, noted for their weaving. A larger percentage are seminomads, moving short distances to summer pastures.

Kurdish society has undergone rapid changes during the past thirty years, so that much of what was written in the nineteenth and early twentieth centuries by Victorian travelers and British administrators is out of date. Tribal leaders in many areas are now a powerless rural gentry or absentee city-dwelling landlords whose children increasingly turn to professions and trades. In the more remote areas, however, the tribal structure still serves a useful purpose.

It is from the areas of Iran and Turkey having mixed tribal and nontribal populations of Kurds that the largest number of quality rugs and carpets have reached international markets. The cities of Bijar and Senneh are particularly prominent due to the facts that rugs for town houses adaptable to

View of a mountainous Kurdish area in Iraq.

Western tastes were produced there for the local gentry and that these districts were more accessible to markets and collecting points, which encouraged production beyond local needs. In Iraq, on the other hand, particularly after the decline of Mosul as a collection center, the rugs and other weavings retained their tribal characteristics of structure and design that, until recently, made them less desirable for the export market.

Iraqi Kurdish Rugs

Kurdish rugs of Iraq are still woven in village or nomadic settings essentially for local use. This means that they are, with few exceptions, made of wool, or wool and goat hair, with warps on the same level, producing flat backs in which each knot appears as two distinct nodes. The pile is medium to long and the knot counts are low, usually from 30 to 60 per square inch. In northern Iraq, the sides are normally finished with reinforced selvedges. Further south, where Persian influences intrude, a figure 8 overcast selvedge is normal. The wool used for reinforcing and overcasting is from batches of colored pile wool forming bands of color along the sides of the rug. The top warp ends are finished with plaits, about 4 by 8 inches, oval or flat, which are attached either to a "V"-shaped braid or a flat horizontal braid or directly to the weft-faced kilim which is usually about 1 to 2 inches wide and of one or more colors. This protects the pile from fringing out and adds the "barbaric" quality noted by Mumford and Hawley. The bottom of the rug may be finished in the same way, or the plaits and flat horizontal braiding may be eliminated, leaving a simple 1 to 2 inch kilim. Both practices are equally common, so the difference is of limited use in classifying rugs according to tribe.

In written reference to the Kurds, much is made of their nomadic traditions. Some authors go so far as to suggest that all Kurds are nomadic. This is far from being the case. Nomadic and seminomadic tribes may have made up as much as half the population in Kurdistan in the nineteenth century, but probably no more than ten percent fit this category now and, as previously mentioned, they account for very few of the rugs reaching international markets from Turkey and Iran. However, in Iraq the nomadic tribes, though small in number, account for an important part of the weaving, and nomadic traditions from the past are seen in the weavings of the other rug-producing tribes.

As far as the Iraqi rugs are concerned, the debate on tribal versus city origins of weaving designs is not particularly relevant, for it is clear that the nomadic requirement for a wide variety of bags and animal trappings has sustained a weaving tradition over many centuries. These nomadic weavings are still the most "authentic," whereas tribes settled in villages for several generations seem to rely more on borrowings and adaptations and, unfortunately, were the first to turn to inexpensive chemical dyes.

The main problem with Iraqi Kurdish rugs, particularly those woven in the plains area near Erbil, is the use of chemical dyes. In the high mountains the use of natural dyes has survived in some villages. However, these are not the clear blues, reds and greens of the Caucasus or of Kurdistan itself a century ago. Instead, dark hues predominate and the reds tend toward reddish brown. The result may be pleasing, but the color palette is limited and does not support the Kurdish reputation for extravagant color sense. When Kurdish women try to employ a variety of bright colors in their weavings, they are obliged to buy dyes in packets in the bazaar, and these are usually the least expensive and simplest types that are neither sunfast nor waterfast. Even the natural dyes may run since they are not always well applied.[4] It has been said that prior to 1948, the dyeing trade in Erbil was in the hands of Jews who were often successful in producing fast colors. Whether these dyes were manufactured with chemicals or natural products is unknown. Dyeing is now a task performed by the same women who weave the rugs. Given the mysteries of the dyeing trade, it is not surprising that their amateurish efforts often result in failure.

In other Kurdish areas, the rugs are not easy to attribute to place of origin. It would be ideal if visits to the bazaars in the principal Kurdish towns would uncover rugs from surrounding rural economic areas. This, however, is not possible. There is no serious rug trade in towns such as Koi Sanjak, Ruwanduz, Akra, Zakho, Amadiya, or even Sulaimaniya. Going from village to village in search of looms is an equally frustrating experience. There are no villages with many looms, and many villages have no looms at all. Hence, persistent inquiries and visits to individual houses become necessary. It seems to be a rule that the more accessible a village, the less weaving is done there. This has meant that the most important and prolific weaving areas have been inaccessible to foreigners for many years and will probably remain so.

However, the search for information on Kurdish rugs of Iraq is not entirely hopeless since many examples can be found in the bazaars of Baghdad and Erbil, and a few are available in Mosul. The rug dealers in Baghdad have only the vaguest idea of where their merchandise comes from, though persistent probings over several years have inspired some of the merchants to ask questions of the jobbers who bring in the rugs. The situation in Erbil is somewhat better since the dealers themselves are Kurds and they are closer to the source of supply. However, visits to the Erbil bazaar are not an everyday occurrence, and even there the tendency is to assign each rug to one of only three or four tribes. Classifying them further has been a painstaking task with far from perfect results. A Kurdish weaver of the Herki tribe accompanied us to Baghdad on one occasion and offered her opinion on the provenance of a number of kilims, rugs and bags. She assigned only half of what dealers called "Herkis" to her own tribe. Another source of information comes from rugs brought by friends from specific villages. These rugs can, therefore, usually be attributed with some accuracy. This research, which is not yet complete, leaves us with the tentative conclusion that it is impossible from a distance to assign exact provenance to most pieces found in the market, though educated guesses can put many of them close to their correct tribal origins.

The Weaving Districts of Iraq

Those dealers in Baghdad who will hazard a guess beyond the simple designation "northern Iraq" usually assign Kurdish weavings to one of four categories: 1. Jaf, 2. Herki, 3. Dizai, and 4. "north of Mosul" or "Jazira." The Jazira (from the Arabic word for "island") is the area west of Mosul extending into Syria between the Tigris and Euphrates rivers; however, little, if any, weaving is done there. The term "Jazira" instead refers to the Turkish town of Jazira Ibn Omar (now Cizre) on the Tigris across the frontier in Turkey. Jazira Ibn Omar was once the capital of the Kurdish Emirate of Bohtan and it has been said that until about fifty years ago, many rugs were produced in nearby villages. To the dealers in Baghdad, these were similar to rugs from further east around Erbil, and as the Jazira production phased out, the label shifted to Kurdish rugs of Iraq in general. The trade terms Jaf, Herki, Dizai, and "north of Mosul" can then be used as classifications that follow roughly four associated geographic regions, although many more than four tribes are involved.

The weaving areas of Iraqi Kurdistan can therefore be divided into four geographical districts: 1. southeast Kurdistan, including Sulaimaniya and the Jaf tribal area; 2. the Erbil plain; 3. the northeast area above Erbil; and 4. the area north of Mosul. These correspond to the trade terms Jaf, Dizai, Herki, and Mosul. It is the second and third categories that account for the largest number of rugs now available.

The Southeast

Straddling the Iraq-Iran border south of Sulaimaniya is the large Jaf tribe, about two-thirds of whom live in Iraq and the rest in Iran. The Jaf tribal leaders, or begzadeh, based in Halabja, have traditionally looked to Senneh (Sanandaj) in Iran for cultural inspiration. However, Jaf weavings are the work of the nomadic sections of the tribe and have none of the refinement of the Senneh productions.

Only occasionally has a Jaf rug been found recently in the Baghdad bazaar. Far more important are the pile saddle bags, often having hooked diamond medallions. These are descendants of the bags transported to the United States by the thousands from Iran and Iraq in the early 1920s. The older bags have clear natural colors of red, green, blue, ivory, and brown, but the newer ones are darker and more subdued, with rust red and brown predominating in what appear to be vegetable dyes. A characteristic of these bags is the formation of the elongated diamond guls by slanting the knots one warp at a time rather than the normal two. Another Jaf sign is the twining and weft float brocade at the edge of the pile. Some of the Jaf bags found in Baghdad are bound together with a very thick and hard overcast of alternating black and white goat hair. Hooked diamond bags are also made by other Kurdish tribes further north, but they are all usually attributed to the Jaf in Iraqi markets.

Weaving activity in the high mountains along the Iraq-Iran frontier in the southeast section is also known, but the important city of Sulaimaniya and the rural area around it now appear to produce few rugs or other weavings. The same can be said for the once important Hamawand tribe between Kirkuk and Erbil. In fact, the bazaars of both Erbil

The plaits at the end of cat. no. 51, a typical feature of Iraqi Kurdish rugs.

and Sulaimaniya are disappointing for those seeking Kurdish textiles, though utilitarian flat-woven Jaf saddle bags are always available. Many of the less expensive Kurdish pieces found in Sulaimaniya are said to come from the Iranian side of the border. In Kirkuk, a few saddle bags and poor quality kilims can be found as well as Dizai pile rugs brought down from Erbil.

The Erbil Plain

The Kurdish tribes of the Erbil plain produce a variety of rugs, bags and kilims. The greatest of these tribes is the Dizai, whose aghas are said to have come into the region from Iran in the eighteenth century to dominate smaller tribes and nontribal peoples. Remnants of these small tribes are still living in Dizai tribal lands and they no doubt account for some of the variety in the rugs.

Although other tribes are probably involved as well, only Erbil area rugs and kilims made by the Dizai, Girdi and Mantik Surchi tribes have been identified. The Dizai pieces stand out from rugs of the same shape and construction made further north because of their bright synthetic dyes. In fact, dealers tend to call any bright rug a Dizai, even though we have discovered that use of synthetic dyes has penetrated the mountains to confound those who seek this characteristic as a simple key to classification. Rug weaving in the Dizai area is to some extent a commercial enterprise, although the market is local. When the rugs have aged somewhat—and it does not take much time—some of them are sent off to the bazaars of Baghdad or Erbil where they are purchased by collectors. Many of the Dizai rugs fit Mumford's description of the "Mosul fabric" because they combine Persian and Caucasian characteristics. On the whole, they are less uninhibited in design than rugs from further north, and are usually more floral, avoiding latch hooks and "Memling" guls. The warp end finishes are often flat plaits and the sides are usually a figure 8 overcast in pile yarn forming color bands.

The Girdi rugs resemble the Dizais in color but most are about a foot wider, giving them a squarish format rarely used by the Kurds. The designs of the Girdis include Caucasian and Turkish elements. Eight-pointed stars and "Memling" guls are sometimes found in the same rug. Most of the Girdis seem to be relatively old, which indicates either that weaving production has declined or current production is in the narrower Dizai format and has lost its separate identity.

Another tribe on the Erbil plain whose weaving can be distinguished from the others is the Mantik. Having broken away from the large Surchi tribe in the Batas area about a century ago, the Mantik brought northern traditions with them in their kilims, bags and rarer rugs. Most of these contain a mixture of natural and synthetic dyes, with relatively small geometric designs predominating.

The Northeast

The most prolific weaving area of Iraqi Kurdistan is in the arc of mountains north of Erbil swinging around to due east. It was here that the great nomadic Herki tribe used to move from winter pastures in the lowlands between Erbil and Akra up to the Iranian frontier and over to the other

A typical eight-pointed star (detail of cat. no. 50).

side where Iranian sections of the tribe are located. Of the rugs and kilims from this area found in the bazaars of Erbil and Baghdad, about half are genuine Herkis. Herki rugs are also found in Turkey, but it is not always clear whether they are woven by the small Herki sections located in Turkey near the Iraqi border or have been brought north from Iraq into the Turkish trade. The Herki rugs found in Turkey are, on the whole, of somewhat better quality than those of Iraq, but whether this is due to the selection process for the market or is an indication that the Turkish sections of the Herki weave better rugs is not clear.

The Herki rug is normally about twice as long as it is wide or 7 by 3½ feet. One end or both are invariably finished with the warps woven in long plaits that are usually oval. Sides normally are finished with flat selvedges in three or four cords overcast with pile wool to form the characteristic Kurdish color bands. In higher quality pieces, the backs are crisp and the designs clearly outlined. The variety of these designs is astonishing. Several are exclusively Herki, the most dramatic being a flower that has taken on an insectlike quality (cat. no. 48). "Memling" guls, latch hooks and geometric medallions are found in all shapes and sizes. A Turkoman type gul is carried in rows much as it would be in a Turkoman rug except that the guls are larger and in outline resemble a Salor variety. "Turkoman medallions" are enlarged and sometimes distorted. There are also borrowings of the four-arm Qashqa'i gul, with the flowers of the field treated in angular Kurdish fashion.

The colors of Herki rugs are usually dark reds, rusts, browns, and blues. These are probably made from plants found in the region, including pomegranate skins. Sometimes synthetic colors are added for minor designs, but the Herki more than the other tribes have continued to use the traditional natural dyes.

Herki kilims and bags are available in many shapes and techniques. A typical kilim in soumak brocade is heavy and single sided since the back is covered with loose yarn ends from the extra-weft wrapping (for examples, see the Dizai kilim, cat. no. 44, and the Herki bag, cat. no. 52). These kilims are found in the typical Kurdish twin panels that in some cases are separated to form two smaller kilims. The Herki also produce many bags, including large double saddle bags in a flat weave that often has four large Kurdish or Turkoman guls. These are sometimes separated by narrow strips of pile. Some Herki bags are entirely pile faced, and these are usually the most attractive because of the use of contrasting light colors along with the dark dyed wool.

Another large weaving group is the Surchi tribe, some of whom are seminomadic. The Surchis are now separated into two sections, with one part northeast of Erbil and the other northwest in the Akra region. Their rugs resemble those of the Herkis, often with lustrous wool in the older pieces. The designs in the Surchi rug seem to be somewhat smaller than in the Herkis, one of their favorites being the notched cross which is found as far south as Loristan in Iran. Only a local weaver could separate the Surchi rugs from those of other nearby tribes. Their kilims also resemble Herki kilims but with less loose yarn on the backs and with smaller geometric patterns.

Iraqi Kurdish rug, Herki tribe, example of "Herki gul" (detail of cat. no. 48).

Although rug dealers in Baghdad and Erbil had indicated that the Barzanis did not make rugs, through friends who visited remote villages in the area it was discovered otherwise. The Barzanis are really a collection of small tribes. Under their Sufi religious shaikhs they have been known for more than a century as the toughest warriors of Kurdistan. The main weaving tribe in the Barzani region is the Mizuri near the Turkish frontier, but the Shirwanis and nontribal Barzanis weave as well. Their rugs are coarser than the Herkis, but similar in many ways, with a mixture of natural and synthetic dyes. Many of the Barzani rugs seem to be copies of Persian or other Kurdish originals, though the designs are strongly rendered.

Many other tribes of this region have also produced rugs and kilims, including the large Pizhdar tribe to the east and the nearby Ako tribe with its nomadic sections—the Boli and Baboli. Further north, the Khailanis used to migrate with the Surchis and Herkis and hence were prolific weavers of bags and kilims as well as rugs. The Balik and Rowandok tribes near the Iranian frontier and the Baradost in the far northeast corner have also produced rugs with considerable originality with the same basic structures as those of the Herkis. Although superficially these rugs resemble one another, a familiarity with hundreds of them reveals an extraordinary variety of designs and originality of treatment.

North of Mosul

The area around Mosul is one of the most interesting in Iraq with its mosaic of Arab Christian and Yazidi villages. The latter speak Kurdish and dress like Kurds though their religion, which features the propitiation of Satan, has drifted a long way from the orthodox Sunni Islam of most Kurds. The Christians are remnants of the ancient churches of the East and still occupy monasteries dating back to the early Christian era when schisms of political and religious origin split the church into a number of separate entities. The Nestorian or Assyrian Church maintains its ancient schismatic traditions; its Catholic counterpart, the Chaldean Church, has for four centuries been reunited with Rome while preserving its Eastern rite in the Syriac (Eastern Aramaic) language. The Jacobite, or Syrian Orthodox Church of Antioch, has its Uniate counterpart in the Syrian Catholic Church.

Kurdistan proper begins about fifty kilometers north of Mosul. There the tribal traditions are less strong than elsewhere in Iraqi Kurdistan. Many of the tribes still have Christian sections, and of these some used to weave rugs and kilims. However, rug weaving now appears to have died out except in a few isolated villages. Rugs from this area have a low knot count with exceptionally flocky wool of the type described by Mumford in discussing Mosul fabrics.[5] These are probably among the descendants of the old Mosuls. The structure is similar to other Kurdish rugs of Iraq with slight variations. Synthetic dyes predominate along with rather degenerate designs. Such rugs do not find a favored place in the market.

Conversely, the quality of kilims from north of Mosul is often very high. Most are woven in a slit tapestry technique with some outlining of designs so that they are not quite identical on both sides. However, most of the kilims do not have the unattractive loose warp yarn found in the Herki soumak technique kilims. Furthermore, the colors tend to be brighter, with white used to accentuate the diamond and latch hook patterns. There appear to be basically two types of these slit tapestry kilims. The first type is similar to the Van kilims made by the Hartuchi tribe in the Turkish Hakkari mountains (some may in fact be made by a section of the Hartuchi, the Gavdan, in northern Iraq). The second type has a horizontal band composition which is usually adorned with weft float brocade.

The pieces included here cover the major areas and structures of Iraqi Kurdish rugs, bags and kilims. However, they provide but a small sampling of the multitude of designs that can be found in this least-known part of Kurdistan. Iraqi weavings never compete on the market or in collections of Kurdish rugs with the more readily available and better-known products of Iran and Turkey. Nevertheless, a survey of Oriental rugs would be incomplete without them.

The best of the old pieces are comparable in dyes, luster of wool and originality of design with rugs of similar age from the Caucasus. These pieces are rare, however, and it must be admitted that the average Iraqi Kurdish piece does not measure up to the tribal and village rugs of the major weaving areas of the Middle East. On the other hand, excluding some of the newer products which are inferior both in dyes and basic materials, the Iraqi Kurdish rugs are solid and attractive examples of a folk art that preserves a weaving tradition that has changed little during the past century. Except in rare cases, the Iraqi rugs have been woven in isolated villages for use by family and friends. Their designs and structures have not been dictated by outside influences or the requirements of the marketplace. Hence, the Iraqi pieces belong with that select group of tribal and village rugs of the East that are the most genuine representatives of a declining art and a changing culture. ໗

William Eagleton, an American diplomat with thirty years of experience in the Middle East, is presently preparing a comprehensive study of the weavings of the Kurds.

Notes

1. John K. Mumford, *Oriental Rugs*, 3d ed. (New York, 1902) and Walter A. Hawley, *Oriental Rugs Antique and Modern* (New York, 1913).

2. Mumford, *Oriental Rugs*, 103.

3. Murray L. Eiland, *Oriental Rugs: A Comprehensive Guide* (Greenwich, Conn., 1973), 43.

4. My own experiments with good quality American weak acid dyes have also led to some color bleeding, but this has been caused by not washing the yarn sufficiently to remove excess color after the dyeing process.

5. Mumford, *Oriental Rugs*, 127.

Slits used in closing a saddle bag (detail of cat. no. 52).

The Kurds

of Turkey

and Their

Weavings

Ralph S. Yohe

*Turkish Kurdish woman weaving on
a horizontal loom.*

Most of the Kurdish cities, towns and villages of Turkey lie east of an imaginary line running north to south just east of Kayseri, with the Soviet Union and Iran to the east, and Iraq and Syria lying to the south. It is in this area, with its high mountain ranges, that the Tigris and Euphrates rivers have their sources. Much of this rugged terrain, although interspersed with fertile plains and irrigated valleys, would be economically useless were it not suitable for use by nomads and seminomads with their flocks of sheep and goats. The survival of the Kurds as distinct tribes with their own language and culture is largely due to the centuries of isolation in this harsh area. Not everyone living in eastern Turkey is Kurdish, however. It is possible to find a sixty-year-old Turkoman village next to a Kurdish village twice that age, and other ethnic groups are also to be found.

A majority of the Kurds live in small farming villages and cultivate the surrounding land. A few may still use wooden plows pulled by oxen and carts with solid wooden wheels, although an increasing number of farmers now use tractors and modern farm equipment.

In summer, many of the villages send their flocks of sheep and goats to high mountain valleys and slopes to graze on the mountain pastures, called *yaylas*. A few families from each village follow the flocks up to the *yaylas* and spend the short summers tending the sheep, growing vegetables and fruit trees, harvesting or planting winter grain while living in small stone or cement block houses or black goat hair tents. In September, the flocks trail back to the fields of the villages on the lower slopes or on the valley plains. Here the flocks glean the recently harvested grain fields.

Farther east, near the Iranian border, families of an entire village may abandon their homes in the spring to migrate with their flocks to the *yayla* leaving only a few old people behind to tend the village during their absence. This is especially true of the Kurds who live in the almost impenetrable mountains south of Lake Van in the Hakkari area where Turkey borders Iran and Iraq.

The Kurdish Weaver

The Kurds of eastern Turkey are among the country's foremost tribal weavers. They have produced some of the Middle East's finest nomadically inspired rugs and kilims. Among the Kurds, the women and girls of the family do the weaving; they regard spinning and weaving as part of their household chores. Other family members, neighbors and friends may drop by and tie a few knots as they visit—a female counterpart to the local tea house where men visit over small glasses of strong, steaming and highly sweetened tea.

The village- and *yayla*-made rugs form an important economic base for the Kurdish family. Just as the surplus milk may be made into cheese to be sold, so the wool beyond that needed for the family's own use is woven into rugs and kilims to be sold. The weavings serve not only as an outlet for the surplus wool at an enhanced price, but they also make use of what would otherwise be surplus family labor.

The Kurdish women traditionally weave on horizontal looms, quite simple in design. (Some weavers use upright looms to make commercial contract rugs and carpets for merchants and large rug establishments located in such rug marketing centers as Kayseri, Isparta and Izmir. Such weavings, while well made, have no place among traditional Kurdish weavings and designs.) The horizontal loom consists of two wooden beams, one at the top, the other at the bottom. Side beams may be used to make a rigid frame, but they are generally used only by town weavers who will have no occasion to move their looms while they are weaving. Warp yarn is wound around and around the two beams. The women may toss a ball of yarn back and forth from one beam to the other as they string the yarn around the beams in a continuous warp. Stakes are driven into the ground to hold the beams apart; sticks wedged into both ends hold tension on the warp.

For ground weft, the weaver often uses as a shuttle a stick wrapped with woolen yarn. The weaver (or more often one of her daughters) generally cuts the knotting yarn into convenient lengths by wrapping the yarn around a wooden rod with a straight slit down its length. A razor blade or a sharp knife is run down the slit cutting the yarn

into uniform lengths. This custom is not used in making large contract carpets and so far as I know, is practiced only by weavers in the Kurdish villages. For kilims, the weaver makes small butterfly bobbins of various colored yarns for tapestry weaving and brocading designs.

The weaver generally pulls the finished part of the rug toward her, wrapping the completed work underneath the beams and bringing the unwoven part forward. Or she may simply sit on the finished part, moving forward as she weaves. If she does not roll the finished part of the rug under the beams as she weaves, when the top side is finished, she turns the loom and works on the bottom side.

The warp threads are manipulated by heddles holding every other warp thread attached to a stick that can lower or raise the warp, making a pathway between the warps to pass the weft threads through. For larger rugs, this stick may be attached to a tripod over the warp to make it easier to pull up or let down the attached warp threads. A second stick inserted in the warp threads behind the heddle raises the other half of the warp when the heddle is let down. This allows the weaver to control the openings for the weft threads so the warp threads cross back and forth over them to make the foundation. The weaver pounds down the weft with a metal or wooden beater purchased in town or from itinerant gypsy peddlers. When the family moves during migration, the weaver pulls up the stakes holding the beams apart, rolls up the unfinished rug and loads the loom and rug on the back of a donkey. It can be set up again quickly at the next location.

Many women still weave designs that are very much traditional, although the designs have been modified over the last few years, often being made simpler. In the small Kurdish village of Ören near Malatya, I asked a weaver where she had gotten the design for a very un-Kurdish looking rug she was weaving. "In books from Germany," was the reply. In some villages, the weavers have given up traditional patterns to weave those dictated by contract rug buyers who generally furnish weavers with both dyed wool and design cartoons.

The weaver of traditional designs usually works in a relaxed atmosphere. An accomplished weaver either makes up the designs as she weaves, recalling a design from memory, or she uses a previously made rug as a model. She occasionally glances at it as she works, changing the design as she sees fit. If an "error" is made, the weaver does not undo her work and reweave. As she works, extra figures may be inserted or changes in the basic design may even be made. Weavers seem to change colors or add new ones almost whimsically. If a weaver runs out of one batch of dyed wool and the color of the second batch does not quite match, what difference does it make? Symmetry and perfection, as appraised by the Western eye, are of no concern to her. In fact, the expert village weaver has a marvelous sense of asymmetrical balance that would do an abstract artist proud; her combinations of colors can be scintillating. The end result can be a rug of rare beauty, the equal, in my eye, of any woven in the Middle East.

Turkish Kurdish flat-woven bag in a soumak wrapping technique (detail of cat. no. 63).

Example of a well-known design in Kurdish rugs of east central Turkey (detail of cat. no. 54).

Turkish Kurdish flat-woven spindle bag with outlining of motifs and twined and knotted fringe (detail of cat. no. 64).

Kurdish Weavings of East Central Turkey

It is an unfortunate source of confusion that a group of rugs woven in the main east central Kurdish areas of Malatya, Elazığ, Tunceli, Erzurum, Diyarbakır, and Adıyaman have long been known in the Western rug trade as Yörük. The merchants in the Istanbul bazaar, however, call these rugs Kurdish and although some of them were undoubtedly made by weavers from other ethnic groups, these rugs are very much based on old Kurdish designs and Kurdish techniques. By the same token, the Kurds must also have borrowed designs from other ethnic groups. Some ethnic Yörüks do live in east central Turkey, but they look upon themselves as being a separate people from the Kurds and are of Turkic origin. Their weavings are very different from real Kurdish examples, with their own patterns, styles and techniques.[1]

Most of the Turkish rugs included here come from the east central area and belong to the Kurdish group. These weavings have certain characteristics in common, a kind of "syndrome," as it were. Not every rug will have all the characteristics, but they will usually have enough of them to make their identification fairly easy.

Many of these rugs tend to be coarsely woven, heavy in weight and "meaty" to the touch. They sometimes pucker and stretch to highly irregular shapes. This results from a combination of the wool warp being stretched with uneven tension and loosely packed wool weft.

In the finer examples, the wool has a high luster and holds the deep-colored dyes well, reminding one of stained glass. Dark brown wool is frequently used for wefting. (The farther east one travels, the more brown-wooled sheep one sees.) Weavers often work end warp threads into wide flat braids and long ropes with a special Kurdish character. Sometimes the ends of the rugs are flat-woven with colorful embroidery added. Weavers may overcast the edges with alternate strands of colored yarn such as red and reddish orange. Or they overcast the two strands to create a figure 8 that encircles the waist of each 8 on the completion of each pass.

In newer rugs, colors seem to be somber. And yet a robust richness can still be found in the coloring of finely made rugs. A lush burnt apricot, generally in the border, is almost a trademark. It is a color one sees in the late evenings in eastern Turkey as the low sun floods the barren brown hills with theatrical lighting. Dark blue backgrounds highlight designs woven in camel brown; a dramatic use of almost iridescent electric blue and clear lemon yellow gives the rugs a special character. Fields sparkle with outlines of white and with wide splashes of bluish green. Mulberry red—another hallmark color—fills large areas. The Kurdish weavers counterplay light red designs against a deep, dark crimson to give a ghost vestige to the pattern.

Wefts are often white, gray, red, or a mixture of colors instead of dark brown. Cotton warps are used in more recent rugs of the Malatya area. Some weavers use regular flat selvedges, sometimes quite heavy, instead of overcasting. Bright and cheerful palettes rather than somber colors appear on many older rugs. Purple—perhaps amaranthine is closer—shows up now and then. In rugs made with synthetic dyes from around the turn of the century or later, purples often have faded to a mousy gray. But now and then one finds a beautiful old rug having a range of purples as its most outstanding color, such as cat. no. 54. Even older rugs may have pinks and bright oranges. Modern Turkish weavers apparently find "electric" pinks and oranges from the chemists' vials absolutely irresistible and scatter them generously through their weavings.

It is more difficult to list the distinguishing features of east central Kurdish kilims. The colors—similar to those in the rugs—frequently point to the Malatya area (cat. no. 56). Cotton is widely used in kilims to create stark white backgrounds to highlight the designs. Designs are generally on a small scale unlike the large flamboyant designs found in kilims of western Turkey. Silver thread often enriches the weaving (cat. no. 64) and motifs are outlined with yarn of a second color.

Large flat-woven bags with strong blues and reds with geometric diamonds and white cotton are found all over the region, but especially large numbers were made in the Sivas area (cat. no. 62).

Soumak brocading (weft wrapping) normally is woven with one or more foundation wefts between the rows of warp wrapping. Kurdish weavers in such areas as Malatya and Gaziantep make soumak brocading with no wefting between the rows of weft wrapping. Such weaving in Turkey is sometimes called "stocking weaving." A bag face (cat. no. 63) provides an example of soumak wrapping without the usual rows of plain wefting between the pattern weft. Distinctive Kurdish characteristics are the strong colors, the compartmentalizing of the designs by weaving techniques and the outlining of the motifs by a separate strand of yarn.

One of the best-known Kurdish designs of east central Turkey is illustrated by cat. no. 54. This rug was purchased in Konya; it is thought to have been woven somewhere in the Malatya area. Some Istanbul dealers identify this design with the town of Cıhanbeyli. I, however, found no such rugs in the main mosque of Cıhanbeyli or in the bazaar and mosques of Malatya. Villages in the Erzurum area did weave such rugs in the 1960s. I purchased in Tokat in 1974 a fragment of what is probably a small bag or pillow of early twentieth century date with a similar design in very cheerful bright reds, blues and white. Since these rugs have been in rather generous supply in the rug markets of Ankara and Istanbul, they were likely made over a wide area of east central Turkey.

Typical view of the mountains largely inhabited by Kurds.

Kurdish villagers in the Malatya, Elazığ and Adıyaman areas still weave stylized versions of the "Holbein" knot.[2] Sometimes the knot is so stylized and crudely designed that one must look a second time to recognize it. Such a knot pattern made up the edges of octagonal medallions in fifteenth century Turkish "Holbein" rugs. They are also woven today in rugs made in Afghanistan. In the Adıyaman area, this design served as the center of an octagonal "pin-wheel" with eight "paddles." The design goes back at least to the fifteenth and sixteenth centuries and is generally attributed to weavers of Ezine in western Turkey. Versions of this basic design appear again and again in the Kurdish rugs of this central area. The most famous of these rugs using the "Holbein" knot are attributed to the small Kurdish village of Pishnik, south of Adıyaman. Until recently, such rugs were certainly woven there and the village is still known for its skilled weavers, but rugs similar to more recent Pishnik weavings are woven in at least two other small villages in the same area.

Farther north, the "pinwheel" minus the center knot octagon has been translated by weavers into "buglike" designs with eight appendages of various sizes and shapes. Weavers in the Elazığ-Tunceli-Arapkır areas wove these rugs at least until recently.[3]

This account of the rugs of east central Turkey, however, does not describe nor mention all of the other various designs found in the east central area, nor does it include several very interesting designs from the area. For instance, I saw several rugs in a Gaziantep mosque bearing designs strangely similar to certain Persian Sarab rugs with camel-colored fields. The same designs are woven in villages in the Ağrı area.[4] A rug in the H. McCoy Jones collection has a field of small repeated stylized carnations in true east central Kurdish colors and technique. I have seen no other rugs like it.[5] Two strikingly dramatic rugs with three shield-like medallions that one would normally associate with Kazak rugs are known to me. The colors, weaving technique and remaining designs are very much those of eastern Turkey. One of the rugs is in the Murray L. Eiland collection;[6] the other is in my collection. Recently, a simplified, somewhat similar design has been woven in the Muş area.

Kurdish Weavings of Southeastern Turkey

A distinctive group of weavings can be attributed to the Kurds living south of Lake Van where Turkey borders Iran and Iraq. This wild mountainous country has few roads. Whole villages spend their summers in goat hair tents following their flocks through the mountains. The men are fine horsemen; many still wear traditional baggy trousers and flowing coats and wrap their heads in white turbans. They carry carbines and are said to be good hunters and expert marksmen. To the unpracticed eye these tribes are practically indistinguishable from the Kurds living across the borders in Iran and Iraq.

The best-known weavers in this area are the women of the Hakkari tribe. They weave coarse-knotted rugs with bold primitive designs and dark colors. Their kilims are also somewhat coarse, woven in two strips on heavy, generally pinkish warp and sewn together. Known in the trade as Van kilims, they generally have a mulberry or dark blue background with overall repeat patterns.[7] Another typical design consists of motifs in vertical rows with alternate reddish and light gold backgrounds (cat. no. 58).

In conclusion, even though some extraordinary rugs are made in southeastern Turkey, the rugs of east central Turkey are surely the best-known Kurdish rugs woven in Turkey and justifiably so. For their sheer beauty of colors, dramatic designs and nomadic character, it is doubtful that they can be matched as a group by any other Kurdish weavings in Turkey. 🙖

Ralph S. Yohe has traveled extensively throughout Turkey. He is a member of the board of trustees of the Textile Museum in Washington, D.C. and has contributed to many of its publications, most recently the catalogue, Flowers of the Yayla: Yörük Weavings of the Toros Mountains.

Notes

1. Part of the following discussion has been adapted from my article, " 'Gone to the Yayla': Rugs of the Yörük Triangle" in Anthony L. Landreau, ed., *Yörük: The Nomadic Weaving Tradition of the Middle East* (Pittsburgh, 1978), 36-38. The discussion in that article included the Kurdish weavings of the area and much of the comment relevant to Kurdish weaving is repeated in this essay. For specifically Yörük weavings, see Landreau et al., *Flowers of the Yayla: Yörük Weavings of the Toros Mountains* (Washington, D.C., 1983).

2. Murray L. Eiland, *Oriental Rugs*, rev. ed. (Boston, 1976), figs. 96-97; Landreau, ed., *Yörük: The Nomadic Weaving Tradition*, pl. 30.

3. Landreau, ed., *Yörük: The Nomadic Weaving Tradition*, pl. 29.

4. One of these is illustrated in Neriman Görgünay, *Doğu Yöresi Halıları* (Ankara, 1970), 97, fig. 73.

5. This rug is now in the M. H. de Young Museum, San Francisco. It was illustrated in the 1982 calendar of the Baktiari Oriental Carpet Gallery, San Francisco.

6. Eiland, *Oriental Rugs*, rev. ed., pl. XLVI (b).

7. Landreau, ed., *Yörük: The Nomadic Weaving Tradition*, pls. 38 and 40.

Turkish Kurdish kilim, Hakkari tribe, with vertical columns of symmetrical devices on contrasting colors (detail of cat. no. 58).

Catalogue Note

ℑ Measurements given do not include fringes. In counting warps and wefts, the vertical figure (abbreviated "vert.") precedes the horizontal (abbreviated "horiz."). Information on the previous ownership or locale of acquisition of pieces is given when available. Unless otherwise specified, the rugs and other weavings have not been previously published.

1

Senneh Rug
19th century

A typical Senneh rug, with an overall field of botehs in brown, red, blue, and pink on an ivory ground. The main border has blue, light green and gold flower and vine motifs on a red ground, flanked by blue guard borders. This rug is also typical of Sennehs in the shortness of the pile and the high knot density.

Size: 51 x 48 in./130 x 122 cm.
Pile: fine, dry wool, Z 2 S, symmetrical knot, short, vert. 15 x horiz. 15 (225 knots per sq. in.)
Warp: white cotton, Z 4 S, no offset
Weft: white cotton, Z 4 S, single shot
Edges: purple silk with little remaining, simple whip; edgewarp: bundle of 4, white cotton, Z 2 S
Ends: cotton, originally white but now tan from exposure; top missing, plain weave at bottom with braided finish
Handle: light
Colors: red, ivory, pink, light blue, light green, gold, medium brown
Condition: good
Provenance: acquired in the New York trade, 1982

Private collection

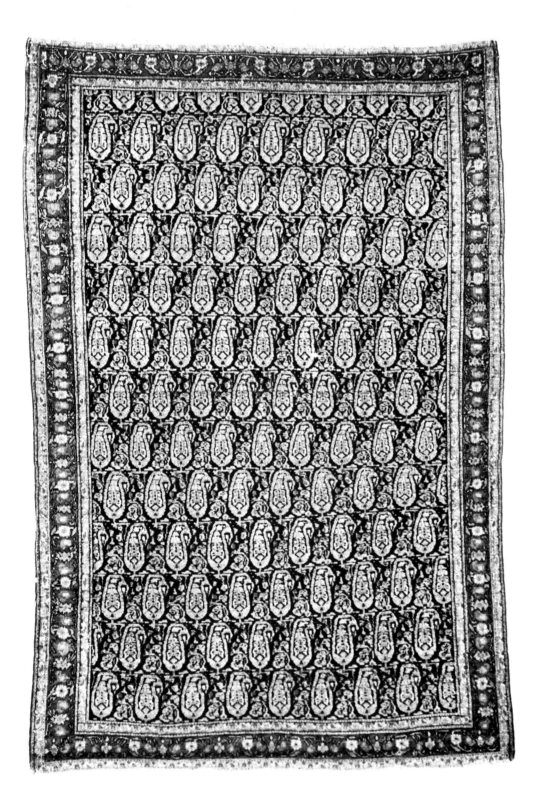

2

Senneh Rug
Late 19th century

The dark blue field of this rug is covered with light green botehs containing red and light blue spots. The border has a red field with light green flowers.

Size: 74 x 50½ in./188 x 128 cm.
Pile: fine, soft wool, Z 2 S, symmetrical knot, short, vert. 18 x horiz. 15 (270 knots per sq. in.)
Warp: white cotton, Z 4 S, full offset
Weft: white cotton, Z 4 S, single shot
Edges: not original; edgewarp: white cotton, Z 4 S
Ends: missing
Handle: light
Colors: dark blue, light green, red, salmon, light blue, white, gold
Condition: some repairs
Provenance: acquired in the Chicago trade, 1979

Collection of Joseph W. Fell

3

Senneh Rug
Early 20th century

The unusual design in the field of this rug consists of green tendrils, yellow and red birds and red-bordered botehs on an ivory ground. The botehs are composed of various colors, including a few spots of pink. The border contains green meandering vines with red botehs on a dark blue ground.

Size: 46 x 39 in./117 x 99 cm.
Pile: scratchy wool, Z 2 S, symmetrical knot, short, vert. 14 x horiz. 10 (140 knots per sq. in.)
Warp: white cotton, Z 4 S, medium offset
Weft: white cotton, Z 4 S, single shot
Edges: not original
Ends: white cotton plain weave at top, macramé on bottom
Handle: stiff
Colors: ivory, dark blue, red, light green, light blue, yellow, medium blue, pink
Condition: very good to excellent
Provenance: acquired in the Chicago trade, 1979

Private collection

4

Senneh Rug
Early 20th century

The Herati pattern throughout the field of this piece presents a fairly typical Senneh design. The central medallion in dark blue with floral motifs in red, pink and light blue floats upon a ground of yellow with red, pink and light blue elements. The inner border is also yellow and contains pink and light blue flowers. The main border is red with yellow and blue elements flanked by blue and red guard borders with meandering vines.

Size: 58½ x 39½ in./149 x 100 cm.
Pile: dull, scratchy, dry wool, Z 2 unplied, symmetrical knot, short, vert. 14 x horiz. 13 (182 knots per sq. in.)
Warp: white cotton, Z 4 S
Weft: white cotton, Z 4 S, single shot
Edges: tan wool, simple whip; foundation wefts extend to edge and are woven over 5 warps; edge-warp: bundle of 5 white cotton Z 4 S warps
Ends: plain weave, red and yellow line of weft twining at bottom
Handle: stiff
Colors: dark blue, ivory, pink, light blue, yellow, green, tan, red
Condition: excellent
Provenance: acquired in 1915 in Sanandaj (Senneh), Iran, by a missionary from whom it was purchased by the present owner in the Chicago area, 1980

Private collection

5

Senneh Saddle Cover
Late 19th century

The dark blue open field of this piece has red spandrels filled with a Herati pattern. The lower half and bottom of the field are bordered in small botehs. The yellow ground main border is flanked by light blue guard borders, both having flower and vine designs. The original slits for the pommel and cantle have been woven shut in a pattern matching the main border.

Size: 38 x 42 in./ 97 x 107 cm.
Pile: dull, scratchy, dry wool, Z 4 S, symmetrical knot, short, vert. 14 x horiz. 15 (210 knots per sq. in.)
Warp: white cotton, Z 4 S
Weft: white cotton, Z 4 S
Edges: not original
Ends: warp fringe
Handle: stiff and light
Colors: dark blue, light reddish orange, light yellow, light blue, light green, pink, brownish red
Condition: somewhat worn
Provenance: acquired in the Chicago trade, 1981

Collection of
Barbara and Roger Hilpp

6

Senneh Kilim
Early 20th century

This Senneh kilim was chosen from
among a large number of available
examples because pieces with dark
fields are less often seen than those
with light grounds. The dark blue
field has an allover floral design in
bluish green, red, white, and rose.
The main border with yellow
ground and the guard borders with
white ground employ variations of
the flower and vine pattern.

Size: 76 x 51 in./193 x 130 cm.
Warp: light brown wool, Z 4 S, 18
per inch
Weft: wool, Z 2 S, 68 per inch
Edges: yellowish green ground weft
returning over outer warp
Ends: yellowish green plain weave,
fringed, twining in yellow and
salmon on both ends
Handle: stiff
Colors: dark blue, rose, pink, light
blue, bluish green, yellowish gold,
red, white
Condition: generally excellent, two
small holes
Provenance: acquired in the
Chicago trade, 1974

Collection of Mary Ann and Ian Lea

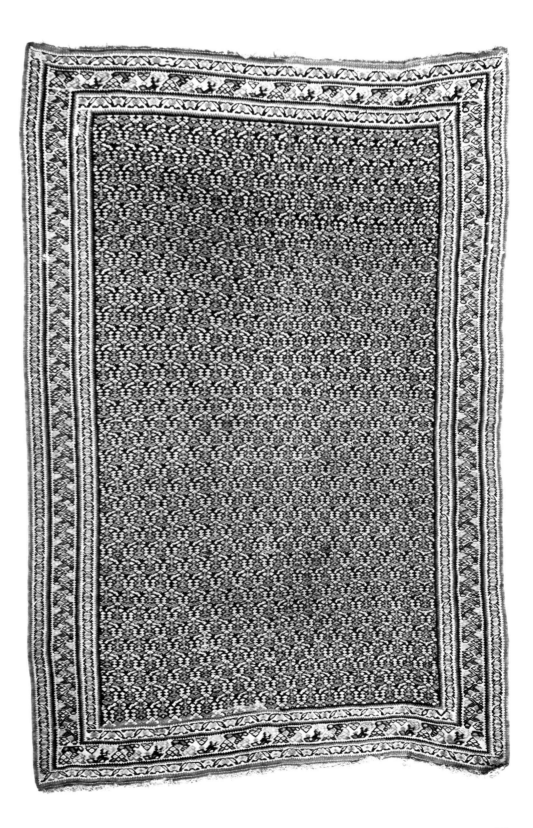

7

Bijar Rug
Late 19th century

The field in this brilliantly hued rug consists of large calices and tulips in various colors arranged in rows. There are vines in ivory edged in light blue and salmon. The border has a flower and vine motif in blue with salmon tendrils on an ivory ground.

Size: 85 x 59 in./216 x 150 cm.
Pile: dull wool, Z 2 spun and 2 unspun strands in each knot, symmetrical knot, short, vert. 10 x horiz. 8 (80 knots per sq. in.)
Warp: tan wool, Z 2 S, full offset
Weft: wool, 2 sinuous Z 2 S and 1 Z heavy cable
Edges: not original; edgewarp: tan wool, 8 warps, Z 2 S in 2 bundles of 4 warps each
Ends: salmon and green wool; 3 rows soumak, 1 row green and salmon weft twining, then 3 rows soumak, terminating in macramé
Handle: stiff, heavy
Colors: dark blue, salmon, ivory, tan, pink, light blue, light green, brown
Condition: somewhat worn
Provenance: bought at auction in Milwaukee, 1980
Published: The Magazine Antiques 120 (October 1981): 774

Collection of Joseph W. Fell

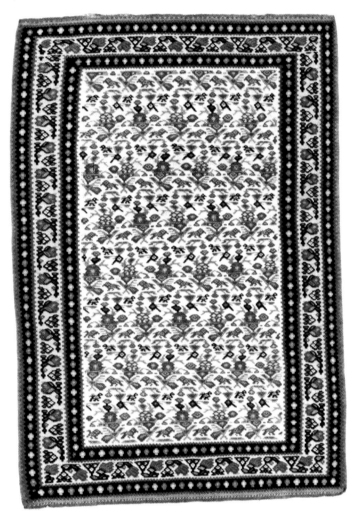

8

Senneh Flat-woven Mat
Late 19th century

This superb piece is unusual in its small size and fineness of weave. The ivory ground of the field is covered with black and brown birds and green chickens. The border has a yellow ground with multi-colored flowers, while the guard borders are black with red and green crosses.

Size: 26 x 18 in./66 x 46 cm.
Warp: ivory silk, S 1
Weft: wool, Z 2 S, slit-weave tapestry
Edges: returning wefts around warp
Ends: ivory silk with macramé panels and knotted warps
Handle: extremely light, loose
Colors: ivory, light green, brownish red, reddish pink, black, gray, yellow, light brown
Condition: excellent
Provenance: acquired in the Chicago trade, 1979

*Collection of
Mr. and Mrs. Wendel R. Swan*

9

Bijar Rug
Late 19th century

The field of this large rug is composed of symmetrical rows of salmon-colored arabesques and stems. The lattice is linked by large vertical palmettes with small horizontal palmette blossoms on a dark blue ground. The large palmettes, as well as the naturalistic sprigs of iris, carnations, pomegranates and other flower and shrub forms are oriented toward the top of the rug. The wide ivory main border contains stylized "turtle" and "fish" elements interspersed with vines and palmettes. The two red ground guard borders have meandering blue and green palmettes superimposed on ivory stems and flowers. The dark yellowish green outer border contains an undulating vine pattern with lotus and carnations. For a similar example, see McMullan 1965, pl. 22.

Size: 180 x 306 in./457 x 777 cm.
Pile: soft wool, Z 2 S, symmetrical knot, medium, vert. 10 x horiz. 9 (90 knots per sq. in.)
Warp: tan wool, Z 2 S, full offset
Weft: tan wool, Z 2 S, 3 shots, 1st and 3d are cables, 2d is sinuous
Edges: red wool, Z 2 S, single whip over bundle of 7 Z 2 S tan warps
Ends: missing
Handle: heavy, stiff
Colors: dark blue, red, salmon, yellow, gold, light blue, medium blue, light yellowish green, dark yellowish green, ivory, bluish green, pink
Condition: generally good, worn down to the knots in several areas

From the Collections of the Evanston Historical Society

10

Bijar Sampler
Early 19th century

This is a very good example of a vagireh or sampler, a piece woven to show to prospective buyers of large formal rugs such as cat. no. 9. The field consists of a salmon-colored arabesque leaf design with flowering trees, plants and small animals in various colors on a dark blue background. On three sides the border has a serrated leaf and flower pattern on an ivory ground. On the fourth side the leaf and flower pattern is simplified and smaller.

Size: 88 x 64½ in./224 x 164 cm.
Pile: soft wool, Z 2 S, symmetrical knot, medium, vert. 9 x horiz. 9 (81 knots per sq. in.)
Warp: tan wool, Z 2 S, full offset
Weft: undyed, ivory wool, Z 2 S, 1 sinuous weft, cable weft has 2 strands in each of 2 shots
Edges: simple whip overcasting in salmon wool; edgewarp: ivory wool, Z 2 S, containing 5 warps in 1 bundle, weft penetrates selvedge
Ends: salmon wool with supplemental weft chaining
Handle: heavy
Colors: dark blue, salmon (abrash light pink to salmon), red, medium blue, greenish blue, light yellow, ivory, medium green, brown, light blue
Condition: some wear in the field and repairs at ends
Provenance: acquired in the Chicago trade, 1980

Collection of
Linda Sandell and David Schwartz

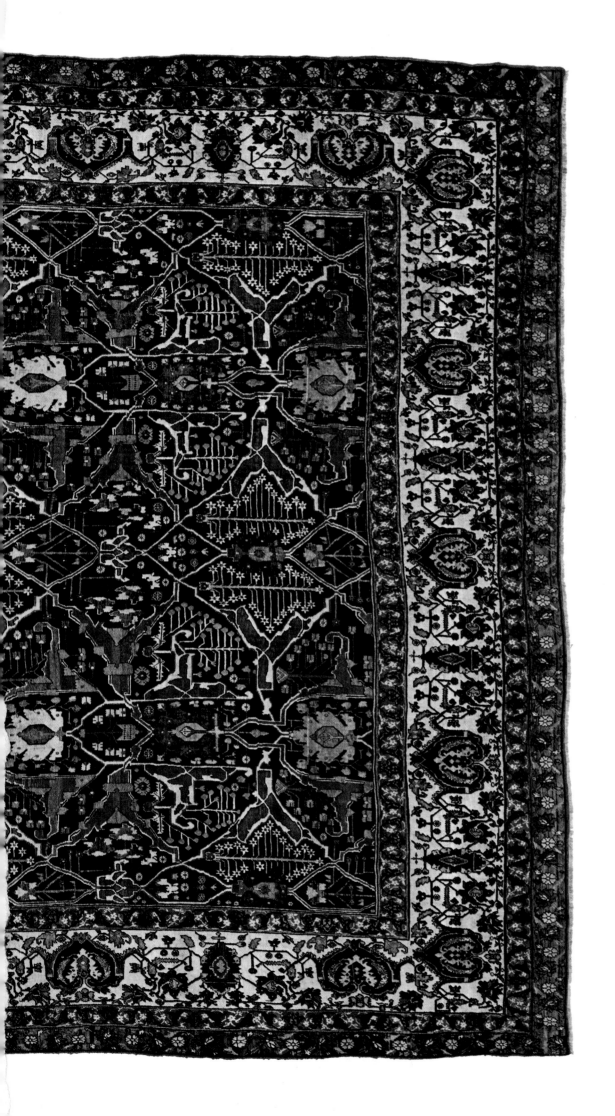

11

Bijar Rug
Late 19th or early 20th century

This magnificent example of a Bijar rug has six intertwined palmettes on a salmon ground forming a small medallion with anchored pendants. The design sits within a dark blue arabesque and vine-covered major medallion also with anchored pendants. The field has an ivory Herati-filled ground. The spandrels are light blue and salmon with vines. The main border is a reciprocating "turtle" design on a dark blue ground. The guard borders are in a flower and vine design.

Size: 92 x 57 in./234 x 145 cm.
Pile: fine, soft, lustrous wool, Z 2 S, symmetrical knot, short, vert. 14 x horiz. 14 (196 knots per sq. in.)
Warp: tan wool, Z 2 S, full offset
Weft: salmon wool, Z 2 S, 3 shots, 1st and 3d sinuous, 2d cable
Edges: salmon wool, simple whip surrounds bundles of 8 tan wool Z 2 S edgewarps; selvedge weft does not penetrate rug
Ends: salmon wool soumak and weft twining; bottom fringe missing
Handle: stiff, light
Colors: light red, dark red, tan, medium brown, dark brown, dark blue, light blue, medium blue, green, ivory, pink
Condition: very good with some low spots and minor repairs
Provenance: acquired in the Chicago trade, c. 1980

Collection of
Mr. and Mrs. Louis C. Krueger

12

Bijar Rug
Late 19th century

The ivory field of this rug has well-spaced floral motifs (harshang pattern) including, near its center, two rows of naturally rendered roses in pink. The floral elements are in salmon, medium brown, pink and blue, ivory, red, and blue. The wide border has a "turtle" design in blue on red. The guard borders consist of a light blue ground with a red and ivory vine and flower motif. The outer border has vines and flowers on a light brown ground.

Among the floral motifs in the center of the ivory field is an Arabic inscription and date. The inscription, the first three lines of which are woven in brown, is part of a poem from the thirteenth century Persian poet Saʿdi's *Gulistan* (*Rose Garden*) written in praise of the Prophet Muhammad. The original verse of four lines reads:

> He attained exaltation by his
> perfection.
> He dispelled darkness by his
> beauty.
> Beauteous are all his qualities.
> Blessing be on him and on his
> family.

In this rug the last line (woven in black rather than in brown) has been altered to read:

> Blessing be upon the seller and
> the buyer.

The rows of roses bordering the inscription are perhaps meant as a visual reference to Saʿdi's poetic work. To the left and right of the poem is a date that reads, "In the month of Suwal 1313" (A.D. 1896). Professor Heshmat Moayyad of the University of Chicago, who kindly translated the inscription, pointed out that the date might also be read 1331 because of the ambiguous placing of the numerals. If the latter is correct, the date would correspond to A.D. 1914.

Size: 75 x 60 in./191 x 152 cm.
Pile: soft, fine wool, Z 2 S, symmetrical knot, very short, vert. 13 x horiz. 10 (130 knots per sq. in.)
Warp: ivory wool, Z 3 S, full offset
Weft: wool, Z 2 S, 2 tan sinuous wefts, Z 2 S, 1 pink cable weft
Edges: tan wool, 7 warps, Z 2 S, in 2 bundles
Ends: missing
Handle: stiff
Colors: ivory, pink, red, salmon, light blue, dark blue, medium green, medium blue, light green, medium brown, yellow, gold
Condition: considerable wear
Provenance: acquired in the Chicago trade, 1979

Collection of
Barbara and Roger Hilpp

13

Bijar Rug
Late 19th century

Made for the Western trade, this rug combines a light brown field with a deep salmon border. The scrolling vines, palmettes, leaves, and cloud bands of the well-drawn field are contrasted with the crowded, European style flowers and leaves of the border.

Size: 96 x 58 in./244 x 147 cm.
Pile: fine, dry, scratchy wool, Z 2 S, symmetrical knot, short, vert. 16 x horiz. 16 (256 knots per sq. in.)
Warp: ivory wool, Z 2 S, very fine, full offset
Weft: salmon wool, Z 2 S, 3 shots, 1st and 3d heavy and taut, 2d fine and sinuous
Edges: salmon wool, Z 2 S in simple whip; selvedge weft penetrates the rug; edgewarp: bundle of 3 ivory wool Z 2 S yarns within a single whip
Handle: stiff and heavy
Colors: light brown, dark salmon, red, light blue, green, dark blue, very light blue, dark green, yellowish green, ivory, light salmon
Condition: edges and ends frayed

Private collection

14

Bijar Mat
Mid-20th century

This very small piece is relatively recent but is an excellent example of modern Bijar weaving. The central medallion has red and pink roses on a dark blue field surrounding a smaller medallion. The spandrels have a red ground with branches of flowers. The borders have a flower and vine pattern.

Size: 22¾ x 33 in./58 x 84 cm.
Pile: soft, lustrous wool, Z 2 S, symmetrical knot, short, vert. 21 x horiz. 17 (357 knots per sq. in.)
Warp: white cotton (machine made), Z 3 S, full offset
Weft: white cotton, Z 2 S, 2 shots
Edges: goldish brown wool, simple whip; edgewarp: 1 bundle of 4-5, Z 2 S white cotton within single whip overcast
Ends: red wool plain weave, weft-twining finish
Handle: stiff
Colors: red, dark blue, pink, green, yellowish green, bluish green, yellow, light blue, tan, grayish green, brown
Condition: excellent
Provenance: acquired in the Chicago trade, 1978

Collection of Michael Isberian

15

Bijar Rug
Early 20th century

The central ivory medallion and
anchor pendants are filled with a
blue vine pattern interspersed with
small vases and flowers. The medallion is outlined in orange and
floats on a light blue background
which is identical in tone to the
outermost border. The spandrels
and inner border are connected
and composed of angular blue vine
patterning on a red ground. Multicolored flower and plant forms are
placed within and among meandering vines. The major border of "turtle" shapes alternating with Herati
patterns on a dark blue ground is
flanked on both sides by narrow
borders of meandering leaf and
flower patterns on an ivory ground.

Size: 108 x 79 in./274 x 201 cm.
Pile: fine, dry wool, Z 2 S, symmetrical knot, short, vert. 11 x
horiz. 11 (121 knots per sq. in.)
Warp: tan and brown wool, Z 2 S,
full offset
Weft: red wool, Z 2 S, 2 shots;
additional sinuous weft in dark
brown Z spun wool
Edges: orange wool, simple whip,
selvedge weft penetrates the rug;
edgewarp: tan and light brown
wool, 4 warps, Z 2 S
Ends: top, tan and brown wool
fringe; bottom, warps turned back
over tan wool heavy cable then
covered with supplemental weft
twining in red and additional supplemental weft twining in brown
and ivory
Handle: stiff
Colors: light green, blue, red,
orange, medium blue, yellow,
ivory, medium brown, dark brown,
light brown
Condition: pile uneven
Provenance: acquired in the
Chicago trade, late 1970s

Collection of Sirak A. Khachikian

16

Bijar Saddle Cover
Late 19th or early 20th century

The colors of this saddle cover are
typical for such pieces; it has a
solid dark blue field with deep
salmon Herati-filled spandrels. The
main border has a gold ground
with multicolored flowers and vines
flanked by light blue borders with a
red flower and vine pattern. The
slits for the pommel and cantle are
bordered by a red and green flower
and vine pattern.

Size: 32½ x 36 in./83 x 91 cm.
Pile: fine, lustrous, soft wool, Z 2 S,
symmetrical knot, short, vert. 16 x
horiz. 16 (256 knots per sq. in.)
Warp: ⅔ cotton Z 3 S, ⅓ mixed
wool and cotton Z 4 S, tan, full
offset

Weft: red, brown and light salmon
wool, Z 2 S; sinuous weft is multicolored, cable is tan and larger; 3
shots, 2 sinuous wefts and 1 pair of
parallel cables
Edges: light salmon wool figure 8
over 6 cotton warps, but overcasting possibly not original
Ends: light salmon cotton and
wool, bottom, plain weave finished
off with warp chaining
Handle: medium stiff, light
Colors: dark blue, gold, green,
salmon, red, light blue, brown,
dark brown, greenish blue
Condition: good
Provenance: acquired in the
Chicago trade, late 1960s

Private collection

17

Bijar Area Village or Nomadic Rug
Early 20th century

The design proportions of this rug are unusual with borders almost as large as the central field. The rust red field contains five compartments, each of which has a large gul. The ivory border has alternating "turtle" and Herati designs. There is a marked abrash in the upper border.

Size: 59 x 38 in./150 x 96 cm.
Pile: wool, Z 2 S, symmetrical knot, medium, vert. 11 x horiz. 6 (66 knots per sq. in.)
Warp: ivory, medium brown, tan, and natural brown wool, Z 2 S, full offset
Weft: light brown and reddish brown wool, Z 2 S with hidden cable weft

Edges: light brown wool overcasting, simple whip, selvedge weft penetrates 1 rug warp; edgewarp: 4-6 light brown warps, Z 2 S, in 2-3 bundles, no cable
Ends: missing
Handle: stiff, heavy
Colors: rust red, ivory, bluish green, medium blue, light yellow, salmon, dark brown, yellowish green
Condition: good, but center low
Provenance: acquired in the Chicago trade, 1979

Private collection

18

Bijar Area Village Rug
Early 20th century

This rug (trade name Kurd Bijar) has a variant of the harshang pattern on a dark blue ground. The colors chosen blend harmoniously to produce an exceedingly successful design. The width and light color of the ivory ground in the main border give a pleasing balance to the colorful field. The large multicolored palmettes and flowers are arranged in five horizontal rows. Between each row is a central angular leaf motif surrounded by flowers, trees, small animals, fish, and human figures. In the lower part of the rug appears a miniature rug in red with details in dark blue and a central ivory rectangle with an imitation inscription. The inner border utilizes light orange in its ground and red in its flower and vine motif to make a graceful transition from the field to the main border. The same colors predominate in the large flowers of the main border. The light blue of the tendrils between the flowers is repeated in the principal colors in the outer border with its flower and vine motif. The repetition of red in the selvedge and kilim ends once again unifies the composition.

Size: 108 x 65 in./274 x 165 cm.
Pile: coarse, dull wool, Z 2 S, symmetrical knot, medium, vert. 11 x horiz. 7 (77 knots per sq. in.)
Warp: tan wool, Z 3 S, full offset
Weft: tan wool, Z 2 S, 2 shots
Edges: red wool in simple whip; edgewarp: 2 bundles of Z 2 S tan wool with 2 warps per bundle
Ends: red wool, plain weave with a line of brown and white weft twining; knotted fringe
Handle: loose
Colors: dark red, red, light blue, ivory, green, reddish brown, medium brown, light orange, yellow, dark brown
Condition: some corrosion in the dark brown
Provenance: acquired in the Chicago trade, 1977

Collection of
Barbara and Roger Hilpp

19

Bijar Kilim
Early 20th century

The dark blue field filled with sprig and flower patterns is enhanced by the soft tan and orangish red crenelated inner guard border. The main border is gold with a multicolored flower and vine motif; the outer border, also crenelated, is orangish red and bluish green. The flowers in the field have petals of salmon bordered in rose, a feature shared with many Senneh kilims.

Size: 117 x 55 in./297 x 140 cm.
Warp: ivory wool, Z 2 S, 11 per inch, no offset
Weft: wool, Z 2 S, 46 per inch
Edges: plain ground weft returning over outer warp
Ends: blue and red weft twining, plum and ivory weft-patterned columns
Handle: stiff, heavy
Colors: dark blue, bluish green, salmon, rose, plum, orangish red, tan, gold
Condition: ends and sides worn, several rewoven areas
Provenance: formerly collection of John West; acquired by present owner, 1979

Collection of Maury Bynum

20

Iranian Kurdish Flat-woven Horse Cover
Late 19th century

This outstanding soumak horse cover is dominated by vertical stripes of various colors decorated with alternating vines and flowers and flowering plant designs. The entire border is red with green and ivory flowers and vines. A strikingly similar piece is found in the Ballard collection (Dimand 1935, pl. 5) attributed to Kermanshah, first half of the nineteenth century (in Ballard 1924, 5 f., the cover was dated sixteenth century). This example is believed to be of Kurdish manufacture, probably of the Bijar area. Kurdish pieces with similar design elements can be found in McMullan 1966, pl. 18 and in another horse cover, Landreau and Pickering 1969, fig. 39. Another piece with a similar border design has been attributed to the Khamseh-Afshar of the Bijar area (Hegenbart 1982, 98 and pl. 29).

Size: 72 x 62 in./183 x 158 cm.
Warp: ivory wool, Z 2 S
Weft: light brown wool, Z spun, 1 shot between soumak rows, 26 per inch
Edges: red wool, simple whip; edgewarp: 4 ivory wool Z 2 S warps in 1 bundle
Ends: bottom, ivory soumak, hemmed; top, warp fringe
Handle: stiff
Colors: red, dark brown, medium blue, dark green, light green, tan, ivory, brown
Condition: excellent
Provenance: auctioned at Archie Shore Galleries, Chicago, 1974; acquired by present owner in St. Louis, 1977

Collection of Michael Isberian

21

Iranian Kurdish Rug
19th century

The field pattern of this piece is a
bold variation of the harshang pattern with yellow, salmon and purple palmettes on a dark blue
ground. The medium blue and bluish green border has connected
geometric designs enclosing a Herati pattern. The white guard borders contain a flower and vine
pattern. The Persian inscription on
the rug reads, "Work of ʿIsmat,
Year 1261." The date, which corre-
sponds to A.D. 1845, may not sig-
nify the true age of this rug, for the
quality of some of the dyes would
seem to indicate a later date.

Size: 178 x 66 in./452 x 168 cm.
Pile: wool, Z 2 S, symmetrical
knot, medium, vert. 9 x horiz. 9
(81 knots per sq. in.)
Warp: white cotton, Z 4-6 S, no
offset
Weft: brown wool, Z 2 S, 1 shot,
low tension
Edges: reddish light brown wool,
single whip over bundle of 2; edge-
warps: cotton, Z 4-6 S
Ends: white cotton plain weave
with green and brown weft twining
Handle: heavy
Colors: dark blue, pinkish red, red,
salmon, light blue, yellow, gold,
bluish green, purple, white
Condition: excellent
Provenance: acquired in the New
York trade, 1979
Published: The Magazine Antiques
123 (March 1983): 502

Collection of Joseph W. Fell

22

Iranian Kurdish Village Rug
Early 20th century

This very colorful rug (trade name Sujbulagh) consists mainly of large Herati patterns on a brown ground. The main border has "S"-forms on a red ground. The inner guard border has a yellow ground with a red, blue, green, and ivory vine and flower motif. There is a similar design in the outer guard border. For a close parallel see the Lefevre rug auction catalogue (London, July 14, 1978), no. 46 (identified as Kurdish).

Size: 93 x 53 in./236 x 135 cm.
Pile: coarse, dry wool, Z 2 S, symmetrical knot, medium, vert. 8 x horiz. 5-6 (40-48 knots per sq. in.)
Warp: tan wool, Z 2 S, no offset
Weft: red wool, Z 2 S, 2 shots
Edges: figure 8 pattern in red wool with ground weft extending into the selvedge wefts; edgewarp: 2 bundles of 4 warps
Ends: bottom missing, top has plain weave and knotted fringe
Handle: loose
Colors: red, ivory, light green, light blue, orangish red, gold, brown, dark blue
Condition: brown corroded, some fold wear, missing outer guard border at bottom end
Provenance: acquired in Milwaukee, c. 1920 by Mary Towner Burnham; descended to Mrs. Mojmir Povolny
Published: Bergstrom Art Center 1979, fig. 18

Collection of
Mr. and Mrs. Mojmir Povolny

23

Iranian Kurdish Village Rug
c. 1930s

The dark blue field is filled with multicolored geometricized harshang devices, botehs, small animals, and flowers. There are two narrow borders of meandering vines; the inner border is yellow, the outer border is blue. The bottom of the rug was begun with a tree and flower design on a white background, indicating that the rug originally was intended to have this pattern (see cat. nos. 19 and 20 for same motif).

Size: 118 x 45 in./300 x 114 cm.
Pile: coarse, soft wool, Z 2 S, symmetrical knot, medium, vert. 9 x horiz. 5 (45 knots per sq. in.)
Warp: dark brown and ivory wool, Z 2 S, no offset
Weft: reddish brown wool, Z 2 S, 2 shots
Edges: machine-made selvedge, not original
Ends: reddish brown wool plain weave with weft twining
Handle: loose
Colors: dark blue, medium blue, light blue, light bluish green, gold, medium brown, bright white
Condition: irregular shape with some wear in the field
Provenance: acquired in the Chicago trade, 1981

Collection of R. D. Biggs

24

Iranian Kurdish Village Rug
Mid-20th century

The camel-colored field contains serrated diamonds and triangles in numerous colors. The border has a gold ground divided into compartments each containing flowers in a variety of colors. The flanking borders have a vine and flower pattern on a red ground.

Size: 74 x 44 in./188 x 112 cm.
Pile: dull wool, Z 2 S, symmetrical knot, medium, vert. 7 x horiz. 6 (42 knots per sq. in.)
Warp: tan and ivory wool, Z 2 S, no offset
Weft: tan wool, Z 2 S, single shot
Edges: brown wool overcasting, single whip over 2 bundles, tan and white wool warps in 2 bundles, the outermost of which has 2 warps, the innermost has 3 warps
Ends: tan wool plain weave and macramé, each end having 2 rows of weft twining in dark blue and pink, light blue and yellow, and brown and yellow
Handle: heavy
Colors: light brown, medium brown, ivory, light green, yellow, light blue, medium green, purple with tip fading, orange, medium blue, pink, gold
Condition: very good
Provenance: acquired in Glens Falls, New York, 1976

Private collection

25

Iranian Kurdish (possibly Lori) Rug
Early 20th century

This is a lively but crudely made and irregularly finished rug (trade name Caucasian). The field has three diamond latch-hooked medallions on a dark blue field. The central medallion is bluish green with red, yellow and blue latch hooks. The field is edged by a reciprocating crenelation in red and blue. The inner guard border has multicolored octagons on an ivory ground. The main border is a "barber pole" in yellow, blue, ivory, and red. The outer guard border depicts rows of lozenges on a ground of dark brown and occasionally dark blue. There is a meandering vine on the lower end in medium blue.

Size: 109 x 51 in./277 x 130 cm.
Pile: soft, lustrous wool, Z 2 S, symmetrical knot, long, vert. 7 x horiz. 8 (56 knots per sq. in.)
Warp: ivory, medium brown, dark brown wool, Z 2 S, no offset
Weft: medium brown, rarely reddish brown wool, Z 2 S, 2-4 shots
Edges: brown and ivory goat hair, blue wool, simple whip overcasting, some "bow tie" penetrating rug; edgewarp: 2 cables, 1 having 7 bundles of Z 2 S wool, other having 11 bundles
Ends: top missing, bottom brown wool, Z spun, plain weave
Handle: loose, heavy
Colors: dark blue, medium blue, bluish green, light red, medium red, yellow, ivory, dark brown
Condition: good
Provenance: acquired in the Chicago trade, 1976

Private collection

26

**Iranian Kurdish Village or
Nomadic Rug**
Early 20th century

The field of this rug is ivory yellow,
filled with irregularly spaced batlike
forms of red, medium green, blue,
and light brown. The inner border
was begun with an ivory ground
but was changed to light greenish
blue a short distance up the rug,
producing a mihrab effect. The
outer border of yellowish brown is
separated from the inner border by
a dark brown and reddish brown
reciprocating crenelation. The bottom border contains a vine and
flower pattern on a green ground.

Size: 86½ x 42 in./220 x 107 cm.
Pile: soft wool, Z 2 S, symmetrical
knot, medium, vert. 7 x horiz. 6
(42 knots per sq. in.)
Warp: white cotton, Z 5-6 S, no
offset
Weft: light brown wool, Z 2 S, 2-4
shots
Edges: machine overcasting, not
original
Ends: reddish brown wool plain
weave with cotton fringe
Handle: loose
Colors: ivory yellow, light brown,
light bluish green, medium bluish
green, red, dark brown, tan, green,
white, reddish brown
Condition: some wear in the field
Provenance: acquired in Fort Ann,
New York, 1976

Private collection

27

Iranian Kurdish Rug
Early 20th century

A field of medium blue is covered by dark red treelike botehs. Triangles on three or four legs are interspersed throughout the field. One row of brown lozenges spans the field. The main border is bluish green with elements of dark red, medium blue and salmon. The inner guard border is ivory with medium blue and red elements. The outer border is ivory with red, green and salmon botehs.

Size: 79½ x 60½ in./202 x 154 cm.
Pile: soft, lustrous wool, 2 Z, unplied, symmetrical knot, long, vert. 8 x horiz. 5 (40 knots per sq. in.)

Warp: ivory wool, Z 2 S, no offset
Weft: pinkish brown wool, S spun, 2 shots
Edges: not original; edgewarp: white wool
Ends: flat weave of 2 wefts in same shed, row of green and brown weft twining at top and bottom
Handle: loose
Colors: medium blue, light blue, ivory, bluish green, dark red, brown, salmon
Condition: patch in left edge, several repairs
Provenance: acquired in the Chicago trade, c. 1975

Collection of Ralph S. Yohe

28

Iranian Kurdish Flat-woven Cover
Late 19th century

This stunning Verneh is notable for the number and brilliance of its colors, the absence of fugitive dyes and color run, the fineness of detail, and the precision of workmanship. The outer border is of medium-fine (16 rows per inch) soumak warp wrapping with a meandering vine and multicolored flower pattern flanked by purple and green crenelations.

Weavings of this type have been variously described as Caucasian, Turkish or Kurdish. This piece is considered to be Kurdish on the basis of its color palette and design features, particularly the flower and vine border.

Size: 117 x 78 in./297 x 198 cm.
Warp: dark blue wool, Z 2 S
Weft: dark blue wool, Z 2 S, single shots between soumak and supplemental weft patterning
Edges: blue wool, plain overcasting
Ends: blue wool, soumak and macramé with cabled and knotted warp fringes
Handle: medium stiff and light
Colors: dark blue, medium blue, tan, green, yellow, light green, brownish green, light greenish blue, dark brown, yellowish brown, white, dark pink, dark purple, reddish orange, red, salmon, plum, purple
Condition: very good
Provenance: acquired in Evanston, Illinois, 1975

Collection of Steve and Barbara Mackey

29

Iranian Kurdish Bag Face
Early 20th century

The dark blue field is covered with various floral elements comprising eight of the nine colors in this bag face. The borders are a vine and flower design on orange and blue backgrounds.

Size: 18 x 19 in./46 x 48 cm.
Pile: soft, lustrous wool, Z 2 S, symmetrical knot, short, vert. 10 x horiz. 9 (90 knots per sq. in.)
Warp: ivory wool, Z 2 S, no offset
Weft: rust red wool, Z 2 S, 2 shots
Edges: one side original greenish blue wool, other side not original, yellowish green wool; simple whip overcasting on 2 bundles of 2 ivory Z 2 S wool warps
Ends: closure slits between red, blue and green wool plain-weave panels at one end, other end missing
Handle: loose, light
Colors: orange, dark blue, ivory, light blue, dark brown, yellow, pink, light green, light brown
Condition: very good
Provenance: acquired in Davenport, Iowa, 1981

Collection of
Mr. and Mrs. Wendel R. Swan

30

Iranian Kurdish Bag Face
Early 20th century

The ground is dark blue with a green lattice design with floral motifs in two shades of rose and blue. The border consists of multicolored flowers on an ivory ground.

Size: 19 x 24 in./48 x 61 cm.
Pile: soft, lustrous wool, Z 2 S, symmetrical knot, short, vert. 12 x horiz. 8 (96 knots per sq. in.)
Warp: ivory wool, Z 2 S
Weft: reddish brown wool, Z 2 S, single shot
Edges: simple whip overcasting in red wool, single ivory wool cable, Z 2 S
Ends: Z spun, unplied red wool plain weave at top and bottom, 2 adjacent warps in the same shed, fringe composed of knotted bundles of 2 warps
Handle: moderately stiff, heavy
Colors: dark blue, light rose, dark rose, light blue, brown, ivory, olive green, yellow
Condition: excellent
Provenance: acquired in Minneapolis, 1981

Collection of
Mr. and Mrs. Wendel R. Swan

31

Iranian Kurdish Bag Face
Early 20th century

Two rectangles, each with a central diamond pattern, one with a blue ground and one with a red ground, form the main design of multi-colored serrated diamonds with pendant crosses, stars, flowers, and animals in the field. The inner border has multicolored geometric flowers on a gold field and the outer border contains multicolored flowers on a blue field. For similar examples, see Bamborough 1979, 105 (identified as Lori tribe) and Saunders 1980, pl. 32b.

Size: 29 x 41 in./74 x 104 cm.
Pile: fine, soft, lustrous wool, Z 2 S, symmetrical knot, medium, vert. 7 x horiz. 7 (49 knots per sq. in.)
Warp: ivory wool, Z 2 S, medium offset
Weft: ivory wool, Z 2 S
Edges: red wool, simple whip; edgewarp: ivory wool Z 2 S, 2 bundles of 4 warps each
Ends: red and blue wool plain weave at bottom, top missing
Handle: medium, loose
Colors: blue, red, gold, greenish blue, ivory, brown
Condition: good, but some fraying at edges
Provenance: acquired in Iowa, 1971

Collection of
Steve and Barbara Mackey

32

Iranian Kurdish Flat-woven
Bag Face
Late 19th century

The fine detailing in this bag face is achieved by use of plain and countered soumak technique. The latch-hooked diamond pattern in the field is composed of a number of colors with ivory used for the central diamond and the smaller evenly spaced highlights. The inner border has eight-pointed stars in various colors on an ivory ground. The main border is a reciprocating crenelation of red and blue while the outer border has geometrical figures in various colors on an ivory ground.

Size: 24 x 28 in./61 x 71 cm.
Warp: ivory wool, Z 2 S
Weft: red wool, Z 2 S, single shot, rows of plain and countered soumak
Edges: missing
Ends: missing
Handle: medium stiff but light
Colors: brownish red, salmon, dark blue, light blue, ivory, bluish green, brown
Condition: good in the field
Provenance: acquired in Davenport, Iowa, c. 1971

Collection of
Mr. and Mrs. Wendel R. Swan

33

**Iranian Kurdish Flat-woven
Bag Face**
Late 19th century

This superb example of the weaver's craft was selected from among several similar bag faces in soumak technique. Such bag faces have been identified previously as Caucasian or Shah-Savan productions. The recent tendency, however, has been to attribute them to the Kurds of northwestern Iran (see Hegenbart 1982, pls. 5-9, 12, 13, 14 and others).

The field has three rows of "turtle" medallions in various colors on a blue ground with a saw-toothed and reciprocating crenelation used to surround the field. A brownish red and light blue "barber pole" forms the inner border. The outer border is composed of dark blue and green lozenges which, at the top and bottom, make up a meandering ribbon on a brownish red ground. The colors in this bag are somewhat unusual in pieces of this type.

Size: 20½ x 18 in./52 x 46 cm.
Warp: brown wool, Z 2 S, tightly spun, no offset, 20 per inch
Weft: ivory wool, Z 2 S, single shot, 20 per inch; pattern weft Z 2 S wool, plain soumak wrapped under 1, over 2
Edges: wool, brown soumak and ground wefts returning over outermost warp; edgewarp: brown wool, Z 2 S
Ends: bottom is red wool, Z 2 S plain weave; the hemmed top is brown plain weave with a band of weft twining; there are green and red panels between the closure slits
Handle: stiff and heavy
Colors: dark blue, ivory, light blue, yellowish green, brownish red, brown
Condition: excellent
Provenance: acquired from the Bahai Temple, Wilmette, Illinois, 1979

Collection of Joseph W. Fell

34

**Iranian Kurdish Flat-woven
Bag Face**
Early 20th century

The soumak patterning on this small, fine piece has an intricate interplay of colors. The field consists of six large serrated diamonds bordered by smaller latch-hooked diamonds. The main border consists of a hooked pattern in medium blue, dark blue and red. The guard borders are a salmon, dark blue and red reciprocating tooth design. At several places on the face there are remnants of silk tufts in yellow, green, dark purple, and white. The dimensions of the piece suggest that it may have been part of a bedding bag.

Size: 36 x 14 in./91 x 36 cm.
Warp: ivory wool, Z 2 S, 18 warps per inch, no offset
Weft: red wool, 56 per inch, Z spun single shot; supplemental weft wrapping composed of 22-24 rows of reverse soumak in Z 2 S
Edges: plain with ground and supplemental wefts returning around a single warp
Ends: red wool, Z spun, plain weave with multicolored Z 2 S bands of weft twining
Handle: stiff and heavy
Colors: dark blue, salmon, ivory, red, plum, green, medium blue
Condition: excellent
Provenance: acquired in the Chicago trade, 1982

Collection of Cynthia G. Curley

35

Iranian Kurdish Salt Bag
Kermanshah Province
probably Sanjabi Tribe
Early 20th century

This salt bag has diamond patterns of predominantly red, brown, green, and blue. The front and the back are quite different. The front is an allover diamond pattern created by supplemental wefts. The back has a more open pattern on a plain tan background with one large diamond in the lower part and another in the upper part. Each large diamond is surrounded by a few smaller diamonds also formed by supplemental wefts. The pile "wear strip" at the bottom is of multicolored flowers on a dark blue ground.

Size: 25 x 13 in./64 x 33 cm.
Pile: soft, lustrous wool, Z 2 S, symmetrical knot, medium, vert. 7 x horiz. 8 (56 knots per sq. in.); pile used in wear strip only
Warp: ivory wool, Z 2 S, 14 per inch

Weft: ivory wool, Z 2 S, 2 shots; front in supplemental weft patterning composed of 3 unplied Z spun strands; back in weft float brocade
Edges: wool in dark red, bluish green and yellow segments with chevron-patterned wrapping
Ends: wool; bottom has a pile "wear strip"; top is hemmed with a chain stitch
Handle: loose, light
Colors: red, brown, blue, dark blue, yellow, bluish green, salmon
Condition: very good
Provenance: acquired in Iran, mid-1970s
Published: Wertime 1979, 44, fig. 13

*Collection of
John and Suzan Wertime*

36

Iranian Kurdish Flat-woven Bag
Khorasan Area
Early 20th century

This intricate bag utilizes the familiar latch hook and serrated diamond motif in brown, gold, ivory, orangish red, and bluish green. Ivory is used throughout to outline the motifs in the field. Separating and bordering the four major medallions are areas with unusual geometric elements in orangish red. The toothed inner border is brown and the outer border has toothed elements on an ivory ground. The panels between the closure slits have similar toothed elements on grounds of various colors. The bag has a flat-woven back of brown and dark brown stripes.

Size: 22 x 22 in./56 x 56 cm.
Warp: ivory wool, Z 2 S, no offset
Weft: wool, Z 2 S, 40 per inch; pattern outlining in ivory
Edges: wool overcasting, ground wefts return around 1 warp
Ends: flat-woven, hemmed
Handle: stiff, medium heavy
Colors: brown, medium blue, bluish green, orangish red, gold, ivory, dark brown
Condition: excellent
Provenance: acquired in New York, c.1960 by W. R. Pickering; by present owner from Mr. Pickering, 1979

Collection of Ralph S. Yohe

84

37

Iranian Kurdish Kilim
Khorasan Area
Mid-20th century

The field consists of a lattice of diamonds with crosses and smaller diamonds in a variety of colors. Each diamond is edged with dark brown and separated from adjacent ones by red and ivory borders. At each end of the field is a band of larger diamonds and latch hooks flanked by a thin band of geometric designs. Both ends have a border of chevron pattern with additional small bands in various colors. Yet another border is dark blue with red "S"-shapes outlined in ivory which is flanked by a checkerboard pattern of yellow and brown on the inside and yellow and red on the outside. At one end of the kilim there is an extra row of supplemental weft patterning.

Size: 126 x 80 in./320 x 203 cm.
Warp: brown and ivory wool, Z 2 S, 14 per inch
Weft: mostly brown wool, red on the ends, Z 2 S, 14 per inch
Edges: simple overcast in brown wool over 3 warp bundles
Ends: weft-faced plain weave with predominantly diagonal extra-weft wrapping; one corner has a single long braid
Handle: stiff, medium heavy
Colors: red, ivory, yellow, dark blue, medium blue, light green, purplish red, dark brown, light brown
Condition: excellent
Provenance: acquired in Tehran, 1976

Collection of Dr. John H. Lorentz

38

Iraqi Kurdish Bag Face
Jaf Tribe
Late 19th century

The diamond lattice pattern in the field is surrounded by an inner border of reciprocating multicolored triangles separated by a chain of ivory rectangles. The outer border has a blue ground with compartmentalized multicolored rosettes. The colors in this example are typical of those found in older Jaf pieces.

Size: 19 x 21 in./48 x 53 cm.
Pile: soft, lustrous wool, Z 2 S, symmetrical knot, short, vert. 14 x horiz. 7 (98 knots per sq. in.)
Warp: ivory wool, Z 2 S, no offset
Weft: ivory wool, Z 2 S, mainly single shots
Edges: not original
Ends: missing
Handle: loose and heavy
Colors: brown, green, bluish green, orangish red, red, plum, ivory, dark blue
Condition: generally good but with a few small holes
Provenance: acquired in the Chicago trade, 1982

Collection of Michael Cuccello

39

Iraqi Kurdish Bag Face
Jaf Tribe
Early 20th century

This bag, in typical Jaf colors, reveals an interesting variation of the diamond lattice design executed in the common technique of adjacent rows of knots tied on alternating warps. The diamonds contain an unusual treatment of the latch hooks; rows of small ivory diamonds are regularly interspersed in the diamond pattern. The border is unusual; the multicolored diamonds and polygons edged in ivory contain "S"- and "Z"-shapes. The marked sculpturing effect is the result of colored areas corroding at different rates.

Size: 21 x 20 in./53 x 51 cm.
Pile: soft, dry, lustrous wool, Z 2 S, symmetrical knot, medium, vert. 10 x horiz. 7 (70 knots per sq. in.)
Warp: ivory wool, Z 2 S, no offset
Weft: blue (2 shots), ivory (2 shots) and red (1 shot) wool, Z 2 S
Edges: not original
Ends: missing
Handle: light and loose
Colors: brown, dark blue, orangish red, red, dark green, dark fuchsia, ivory, medium blue, yellowish green, gold
Condition: excellent
Provenance: acquired in Evanston, Illinois, 1971

Collection of
Steve and Barbara Mackey

Iraqi (?) Kurdish Bag Face
Jaf Tribe
Early 20th century

The pattern is predominantly dark blue diamonds with latch hooks on multicolored diamond shapes outlined by dashes of ivory. The multiple borders are in a number of colors and motifs. The unusually large skirt consists of alternating rows of rosettes in red on green and green on red. The general color palette resembles that of a Baluchi rug. It may be that this piece should be attributed to the remnant of the Jaf tribe in western Iran. However, similar pieces can be seen in the Baghdad bazaar, suggesting an Iraqi Jaf origin.

Size: 29 x 45 in./74 x 114 cm.
Pile: coarse, soft, lustrous wool, Z 2 S, symmetrical knot, short, vert. 7 x horiz. 7 (49 knots per sq. in.)
Warp: ivory wool, Z 2 S, no offset
Weft: ivory wool, Z 2 S, 2 or 3 shots
Edges: not original; dark blue wool, simple whip, selvedge weft penetrates rug, warp is wool, 1 bundle of 6 strands
Ends: missing
Colors: ivory, tan, brownish green, brownish red, dark blue, light orange, dark green, brown
Condition: good, several repairs
Provenance: acquired in Evanston, Illinois, 1976

Collection of
Steve and Barbara Mackey

41

Iraqi (?) Kurdish Bag Face
Jaf Tribe (?)
Early 20th century

Decorated skirt and closure slits and occasional crosses within the diamonds of its overall pattern characterize this bag face. The borders are ivory, red and blue with diamonds and rosettes in various colors. Between the main field and the flat-woven skirt with its supplemental weft-patterned chevrons is a band of interlocking "S"-shapes in various colors. Because of its color palette and the supplemental weft patterning, unusual in a Jaf piece, this bag face could be considered Turkish Kurdish in origin.

Size: 41 x 45 in./104 x 114 cm.
Pile: soft, fine, lustrous wool, Z 2 S, symmetrical knot, long, vert. 10 x horiz. 5 (50 knots per sq. in.)
Warp: ivory wool, Z 2 S, no offset
Weft: ivory and red wool, Z 2 S, 2 shots
Edges: brownish red wool, Z 2 S, simple whip with weft penetrating the rug; the transition of the ground weft to the selvedge is unusual in that often the red wefting floats over 3-5 warps; edgewarp: ivory wool, Z 2 S, 10 warps in 1 bundle
Ends: bottom, brown flat weave with bands of multicolored supplemental weft patterning; top, plain weave panels of various colors between the closure slits
Handle: heavy and loose
Colors: red, orange, yellowish green (abrash), ivory, plum, brown, dark blue, salmon
Condition: excellent
Provenance: acquired in the Chicago trade, 1978

Collection of
Mr. and Mrs. Wendel R. Swan

42

Iraqi Kurdish Rug
Dizai Tribe
Mid-20th century

This rug exhibits the typical characteristics of pieces made by the Dizai tribe with its unstable dyes, predominance of orange, flat end plaits, and the figure 8 overcast edges. The design is also typical, with a cornered rectangular center field, medium-sized guls, and small devices placed with some symmetry. There is a liberal use of pink in the guls and other elements. The reciprocal crenelated border in green, orange and red is, however, unusual, as is the middle border with a "running dog" motif in a variety of colors on an ivory ground. Only the outer border, with its geometric rosettes on a red ground, is standard. Since Iraqi Kurdish rugs are uniformly flat-backed, the slight depression of alternate warps is also noteworthy.

Size: 84 x 44 in./213 x 112 cm.
Pile: dry wool, Z 2 S, symmetrical knot, long, vert. 7 x horiz. 5 (35 knots per sq. in.)
Warp: tan and ivory wool, Z 2 S, slight offset
Weft: medium brown and dark brown goat hair, Z 2 S, 2-4 shots
Edges: figure 8 overcasting in the same wool as the pile, Z 2-4 S, forming bands of color; 2 bundles of tan and brown wool, Z 2 S, 2 warps each
Ends: top, plain weave with short, flat plaits where intact, otherwise fringe only; bottom, 2 inch weft-faced plain weave with warps plaited flat and running along the end
Colors: orange, red, dark red, pink, purple, light purple, gray, dark blue, ivory
Condition: generally good, but some repairs and considerable fading
Provenance: acquired in Iraq, c. 1981

Collection of William Eagleton

43

Iraqi Kurdish Kilim
Surchi Tribe
Mid-20th century

This kilim is one of an originally
joined pair. It has interlocking
chevrons and diamonds in slit
weave and "I"-shapes in an aus-
tere, limited color range. Kilims of
this type have sometimes been
confused with kilims from Afghanistan where chevron patterns are
also used extensively.

Size: 76 x 26 in./193 x 66 cm.
Warp: bands of bluish green and
salmon wool, Z 2 S, 11 per inch
Weft: wool, Z 2 S, 5-6 per inch;
plain soumak panels, wrapped
under 1, over 2, with dark blue
ground wefts
Edges: plain, ground weft returns
over outer warp
Ends: one end hemmed, the other
in a plain weave
Handle: stiff and heavy
Colors: brownish red, black, dark
green, ivory, orange
Condition: good
Provenance: acquired in Baghdad,
1978

Collection of McGuire Gibson

44

Iraqi Kurdish Kilim
Dizai Tribe
Mid-20th century

The somber effect of the brownish
red and blue in this kilim is offset
by the use of white, ivory and gold
elements. The two large medallions in the center are outlined in
white cotton. The latch-hooked
diamond motif is used extensively
in the background. As in cat. no.
43, this piece is one of a pair originally joined into a single piece.

Size: 88 x 37 in./224 x 94 cm.
Warp: ivory wool, Z 2 S, 11 per
inch
Weft: wool, Z 2 S, 5-6 per inch,
and white cotton
Edges: plain, ground weft returns
over outer warp
Ends: plain, with fringes of knotted
bundles of 2-3 warps at top,
bottom hemmed
Handle: stiff, heavy
Colors: brownish red, blue, rust
brown, ivory, tan, gold, white
highlights of natural cotton
Condition: excellent
Provenance: acquired in Baghdad,
1978

Collection of James McNeill Mesplé

45

Iraqi Kurdish Rug
Surchi Tribe
Mid-20th century

The good dyes in this fine rug are unusual for a modern Iraqi piece. In a local bazaar it would probably be attributed to the large, nomadic Herki tribe. However, the leaf and wine glass border is rendered in the manner of the Surchi tribe. The field is dark blue and has several different geometric and plant forms in a variety of colors. There are four human figures in red in the lower middle area. The upper and lower medallions are rectangles with projecting arms. The middle medallions are diamonds, one with an outline of ivory latch hooks, the other with a serrated edge of green and red. The leaf and wine glass motif is in blue, green, red, and orange. The outer border of geometric multicolored flowers is on a purplish red ground. The main design is often found in Karaja rugs woven by Azerbaijani Turks. It is difficult to determine whether it was originally a Kurdish or a Turkish adaptation of an older floral design.

Size: 98 x 42 in./249 x 107 cm.
Pile: soft, lustrous wool, Z 2 S, symmetrical knot, medium, vert. 8 x horiz. 5 (40 knots per sq. in.)
Warp: orange and faded plum mohair, Z 2 S, no offset
Weft: dark brown goat hair, Z 2 S, 2 shots
Edges: figure 8 overcasting in purplish red, dark blue and orange wool identical to that in the pile forming colored bands; edgewarp: mohair in 3 bundles of 2 warps each
Ends: top, 2 inch plain weave of purplish red and blue stripes, warps macraméed into "V"-shaped braids, terminating in long plaits, some with fringe; bottom, 4 inch weft-faced kilim in purplish red and dark blue stripes, one line of ivory and red weft twining; warp fringe plaited along end of kilim
Handle: loose, heavy
Colors: medium blue, dark blue, green, red, orange, ivory, purplish red
Condition: excellent
Provenance: acquired in Iraq, c. 1981

Collection of William Eagleton

46

Iraqi Kurdish Flat-woven Salt Bag
Surchi Tribe, Mantik Branch
Mid-20th century

Although tattered, this piece is a rare example of an Iraqi salt bag. The front and back are covered with soumak patterning, the former in a diamond lattice with a saw-toothed border. The lattice is in red, peach, ivory, and shades of brown while the border is in peach and blue separated by red. The back has bands of purple, yellow, blue, and red soumak. There is a "wear strip" at the bottom in weft float patterning.

Size: 29 x 17 in./74 x 43 cm.
Warp: tan wool, Z 2 S, 8 per inch

Weft: ground weft on the front is dark blue single Z spun wool, on the back it is tan wool single Z spun, both with supplemental weft float patterning
Edges: chevron overcast side seam in Z 2 S brown goat hair
Ends: hemmed, not original
Handle: stiff, coarse
Colors: ivory, purple, yellow, blue, red, peach, brown
Condition: tattered, pattern weft damaged
Provenance: acquired in Baghdad, 1976

Collection of McGuire Gibson

47

Iraqi Kurdish Pile and Flat-woven Bag Face
Herki Tribe
Early 20th century

There are six panels in soumak technique separated from one another by bordering strips of pile. Each soumak panel has a lozenge with fuchsia as the predominant color. The pile border has a stylized flower and vine motif. For similarities in the treatment of minor details, see cat. no. 36.

Size: 31 x 32 in./79 x 81 cm.
Pile: dull, coarse, dry wool, Z 2 S, symmetrical knot, medium, vert. 8 x horiz. 5 (40 knots per sq. in.)
Warp: ivory wool, Z 2 S, no offset
Weft: light brown wool, Z spun, 2-4 shots; 14 rows of soumak per inch; wefts in soumak areas do not all extend into pile area; soumak is Z 2 S wool
Edges: wool overcasting in figure 8; Z 2 S supplemental weft extends to outermost warp; edgewarp: 4 bundles of 2 unplied warps
Ends: blue wool plain weave at bottom, top missing
Handle: medium stiff, heavy
Colors: dark blue, light blue, ivory, pink, fuchsia
Condition: worn and slightly faded
Provenance: acquired in Baghdad, 1974

Collection of McGuire Gibson

Iraqi Kurdish Rug
Herki Tribe
Mid-20th century

The central design in this rug is woven only by the Herki tribe, thus the gul might be called the "Herki gul." It appears on pile and flat-woven bags as well as on kilims. Though obviously of floral origin, it has taken on an insectlike quality. The medallions rest on a field of purplish red which has scattered star and plant elements in blue, orange, red, ivory, and pink. The multicolored guls and the connecting bars have an ivory ground. The three borders all have the same pattern of star-shaped flower and vine motif, although on grounds of differing colors. This rug is unusual for a Herki piece because it does not end in plaited warps. Instead, it has a flat band of braiding made from the warps which continue as an unusually long fringe. Typical of Herki rugs, however, is the figure 8 overcasting and the bands of color on the edges.

Size: 89 x 42 in./226 x 107 cm.
Pile: lustrous wool, Z 2 S, symmetrical knot, medium, vert. 5-7 x horiz. 5 (25-35 knots per sq. in.)
Warp: mohair, Z 2 S, in dark brown, black, orange, plum, ivory, no offset
Weft: dark brown goat hair or mohair, 3-4 shots
Edges: figure 8 overcasting in same wool as the pile, Z 2 S, over 5 bundles; edgewarp: 5 bundles of 2 Z 2 S warps each
Ends: top, dark brown and red striped weft-faced kilim with line of dark brown and white twining ending in a multicolored flat braid formed from the warps, then a long fringe; bottom, 3 inch dark brown weft-faced plain weave with a line of red and blue twining; warps of various colors formed into a flat braid and fringe
Handle: loose and heavy
Colors: dark red, purplish red, dark blue, medium blue, orange, ivory, brown
Condition: excellent
Provenance: acquired in Iraq, c. 1981

Collection of William Eagleton

49

Iraqi Kurdish Rug
Herki Tribe
Mid-20th century

The double-paneled central design in this rug is of a type usually associated with the Megri or Rhodes rugs of southwestern Turkey. The panels end in points and have red fields on which are diamonds in dark blue, ivory and red, surrounded by small stars in green and blue. The ivory edging forms latch hooks at both ends. The area between the panels is composed of rectangles with multicolored diamonds and stars. The inner and outer "running dog" borders are in different combinations of dark blue, ivory and red. The main border is orange with multicolored diamonds and geometric flowers. The entire rug has a small outer border of red and dark blue checks. The somber colors in this rug are probably from natural dyes.

Size: 80 x 42 in./203 x 107 cm.
Pile: wool, Z 2 S, symmetrical knot, medium, vert. 5-7 x horiz. 5 (25-35 knots per sq. in.)
Warp: predominantly ivory wool, Z 2 S, with some groups of light red warps, no offset
Weft: dark brown goat hair, S spun, 2-4 shots
Edges: figure 8 overcasting in the same wool as the pile, Z 3-4 S, forming bands of color; edgewarp: 4 bundles of 2 Z 2 S warps
Ends: top, weft float kilim in brown and dark red stripes with red and white weft twining, warps macraméed into "V"-shaped braids, then long round plaits; bottom, same as top with blue kilim
Handle: loose, heavy
Colors: dark red, orange, dark blue, bluish green, ivory, brown, gray
Condition: excellent
Provenance: acquired in Iraq, c. 1981

Collection of William Eagleton

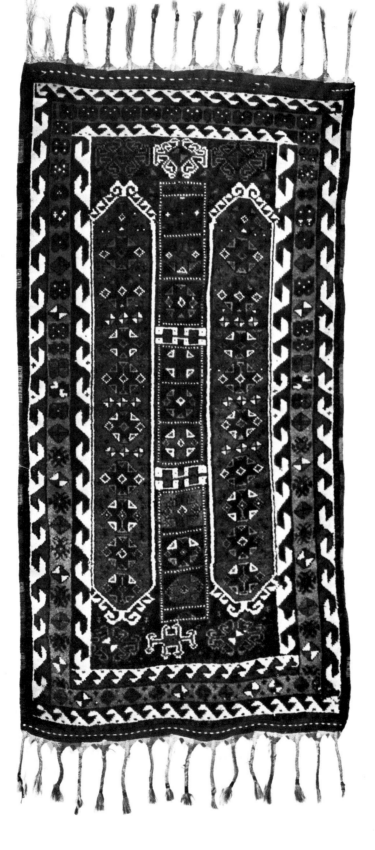

Iraqi Kurdish Rug
Herki or Girdi Tribe
Early 20th century

This is a type of rug that a Herki
weaver attributed to her own tribe.
If this is a correct attribution, the
weaver of this and similar pieces
has chosen to use the wide format
usually associated with the Girdi
tribe north of Erbil. The nomadic
Herki often winter near the Girdi,
which might account for the similarity in design and format. Rugs
of this type combine stars and
"Memling" guls in the center and a
wide ivory ground main border
with a "V" inside the wine glass of
the leaf and wine glass design.
Multicolored stars are enclosed in
rectangular compartments throughout the field. One compartment in
the lower left has an orange field
with two birds in light blue, dark
blue and red. The top of the field
has a row of smaller compartments
with "X"-shapes rather than stars.

Size: 71 x 51 in./180 x 130 cm.
Pile: coarse, lustrous wool, Z 2 S,
symmetrical knot, long, vert. 6 x
horiz. 3 (18 knots per sq. in.)
Warp: ivory wool, Z 2 S, medium
offset
Weft: dark brown goat hair, Z 2 S,
2-3 shots
Edges: figure 8 overcasting in Z 3-4
S wool forming bands of orange,
red, blue, purple, and brown, some
simple whip overcasting in same
colors not original
Ends: top, 1 inch striped brown
and blue plain weave with warp
macraméed into "V"-shaped
braids; bottom, simple fringe with
evidence of dyeing, possibly indicating an original kilim end, now
missing
Handle: heavy and loose
Colors: dark brown, medium blue,
dark blue, greenish blue, ivory,
light purple, dark purple, light
brown, dark red, light red, orange,
gray
Condition: very good, tip fading,
shortened at lower end
Provenance: acquired in Iraq,
c. 1981

Collection of William Eagleton

51

Iraqi Kurdish Rug
Khailani Tribe
Mid-20th century

Although a Herki weaver attributed this rug to the nomadic Khailani tribe that winters near Harir east of Erbil, in the local bazaars it would probably be called a Herki, along with most other nomadic weavings of northeastern Iraq. In rugs of this type, the guls often crowd out the side borders. This piece uses a limited number of colors in a variety of shades and combinations; the guls are very dark blue, medium blue, orange, and purplish red and seem to float on the ivory ground. In two guls there are human figures in gold and ivory. The use of orange as the predominant color in the borders and the central staff serves to unify the composition.

Size: 78 x 50 in./198 x 127 cm.
Pile: coarse, dry wool and mohair, Z 2 S, symmetrical knot, medium, vert. 6 x horiz. 4 (24 knots per sq. in.)
Warp: ivory mohair, Z 2 S, no offset
Weft: black goat hair, Z 2 S, 2-6 shots
Edges: figure 8 overcasting, Z 4 S wool in same colors as in the pile forming bands of color; edgewarp: 3 bundles of Z 2 S ivory mohair
Ends: top, 2 inch black and purplish red plain weave with 2 lines of supplemental weft twining, warps made into "V"-shaped braids, then into flat plaits; bottom, purplish red plain weave with flat or oval plaits wrapped at ends with pile wool
Handle: loose and heavy
Colors: dark blue, ivory, purplish red, orange, medium blue, gold, yellow, orange
Condition: good but repaired on left edge
Provenance: acquired in Iraq, c. 1981

Collection of William Eagleton

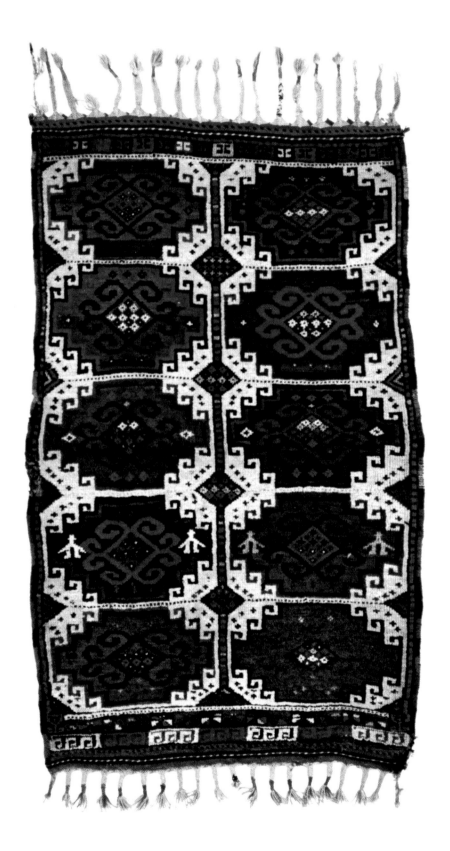

52

Iraqi Kurdish Flat-woven Bag
Herki or Surchi Tribe
c. 1970s

This bag (trade name Jezirah) uses horizontal bands on the soumak face with latch-hooked diamonds in the two broader bands. The smaller bands have serrated rectangles and latch-hooked designs. The colors are unusually vivid. The panels between the closure slits seem even brighter because they are solid blocks of color. There are braided loops for closure. The back has multicolored stripes in plain weave. The quantity of long, loose yarns on the back of this piece is typical of Herki flat weaves, but is also seen in Dizai pieces such as cat. no. 44, a kilim.

Size: 57 x 29 in./145 x 74 cm.
Warp: ivory wool, Z 2 S, 11 per inch
Weft: wool, Z 2 S
Edges: wool overcasting in figure 8, 4 warps per bundle
Ends: hemmed
Handle: stiff, heavy
Colors: red, light blue, pink, green, ivory, orange, plum, dark blue
Condition: excellent, side bindings missing
Provenance: acquired in Iraq, 1976

Collection of R. D. Biggs

53

Turkish Kurdish Rug
Early 20th century

This rug has seven panels with latch-hooked diamond devices outlined with ivory inner borders. The main border has alternating triangles in blue, orangish red and ivory. The outer border has ivory, red and blue "S"- forms. Rugs of this type have often been misattributed as Yörük.

Size: 96 x 48 in./244 x 122 cm.
Pile: coarse, lustrous wool, Z 2 S, symmetrical knot, medium, vert. 9 x horiz. 11 (99 knots per sq. in.)
Warp: ivory wool, Z 2 S
Weft: very dark wool, Z 2 S, 2 shots
Edges: wool, partly original, red and plum on the left side, red and blue alternating on the right in a "bow tie" pattern; areas not original are overcast in plum wool; edgewarp: 2 bundles of 2 warps each, Z 2 S
Ends: red wool, plain weave, knotted fringe
Handle: heavy and loose
Colors: orangish red, ivory, plum, blue green, dark blue
Condition: excellent
Provenance: acquired in the San Francisco trade, 1980

Collection of
Mr. and Mrs. Wendel R. Swan

54

Turkish Kurdish Rug
Malatya Area (?)
Late 19th century

The field in this striking rug consists of a latch-hooked diamond pattern in light salmon within which are placed rows of similar latch-hooked diamonds in various colors. The main border, in the same colors as the field, has repeated symmetrical hooked devices. A similar rug can be seen in Oettingen 1921, vol. 2, pl. 11, attributed to eastern Anatolia and given the trade name "Sultan." Housego 1978, pl. 61, illustrates a similar rug and suggests an origin in western Iranian Kurdistan, mentioning the Sanjabi or Jaf Kurds, and points out that such pieces are sometimes sold under the trade name of Mosul.

Size: 192 x 48 in./488 x 122 cm.
Pile: fine, soft, lustrous wool, Z 2 S, symmetrical knot, medium, vert. 8 x horiz. 6 (48 knots per sq. in.)
Warp: ivory wool, Z 2 S, no offset
Weft: red wool, Z spun, 4 shots
Edges: blue, salmon and red alternating segments in figure 8 overcasting; edgewarp: ivory wool, Z 2 S, 2 bundles, 2 warps per bundle
Ends: red wool, Z spun, plain weave
Handle: medium
Colors: light salmon, salmon, dark blue, medium blue, greenish blue, violet, medium brown, dark brown, ivory, plum (abrash in blues)
Condition: good, but only part of the flat weave at ends preserved
Provenance: acquired in Konya, Turkey, 1980

Collection of Ralph S. Yohe

55

Turkish Kurdish Bedding Rug
Early 20th century

The long pile of this piece is typical of bedding rugs (Turkish *yatak*) made for domestic use. The field consists of four rows of squares containing guls within a gold border that has stiff geometric "S"-forms. The top and bottom panels are a multicolored shieldlike motif. It is difficult to attribute this piece precisely. The colors strongly suggest the Malatya area although the shield motifs at the ends are typical of rugs of the Konya basin.

Size: 64 x 51 in./163 x 130 cm.
Pile: coarse, soft, lustrous wool, Z 2 unplied, symmetrical knot, very long, vert. 6 x horiz. 6 (36 knots per sq. in.)
Warp: wool, Z 2 S, no offset
Weft: brown wool, Z unplied, 2 shots
Edges: brown wool, figure 8 overcasting, 4 bundles of 2 warps each; edgewarp: ivory wool, Z 2 S, 8 bundles of 2 unplied warps each
Ends: bottom has 2 inches of ivory and brown striped plain weave with warps around a heavy cable, top is brown plain weave
Handle: loose, heavy
Colors: red, pinkish red, green, gold, medium blue, ivory, dark brown
Condition: excellent
Provenance: Nahigian Bros., Chicago, inventory, 1916; acquired by present owner, 1978

Collection of
Mr. and Mrs. Wendel R. Swan

56

Turkish Kurdish Kilim
Malatya Area
Late 19th or early 20th century

This extraordinarily pleasing kilim in two joined pieces is divided into nine horizontal panels in various colors. The panels are filled with diamonds, hourglass forms and other geometric shapes. The toothed border in orange has diamond-shaped elements.

Size: 123 x 68 in./312 x 173 cm.
Warp: ivory and brown wool, Z 2 S, 10 per inch
Weft: wool and white cotton, Z 2 S, 64 per inch; single stitching in soumak technique outlines the design
Edges: ground weft returns over 1 warp
Ends: undyed wool tied in macramé with tassels
Handle: stiff
Colors: light reddish orange, dark blue, orangish salmon, bluish green, purplish brown, light brown, white (in cotton), light yellow, fuchsia
Condition: very good
Provenance: acquired in the Chicago trade, 1979

Collection of Ralph S. Yohe

57

Turkish Kurdish Rug
Early 20th century.

The allover field pattern of this rug is serrated diamonds in a variety of colors. The main border has a red ground separated into compartments with floral and "S"-patterns. The guard borders are also on a red ground with an ivory "running dog" pattern. There is a degree of uncertainty about the attribution of rugs of this type. This piece was identified as Yörük when previously published. An Iranian Kurdish origin has also been suggested.

Size: 110 x 51 in./279 x 130 cm.
Pile: coarse, dry wool, Z 2 S, symmetrical knot, medium, vert. 8 x horiz. 6 (48 knots per sq. in.)
Warp: ivory wool, Z 2 S, slightly offset
Weft: brown wool, Z 2 S, 3-4 shots
Edges: wool in gold, greenish blue, orangish red, dark blue, green, medium blue (color changes every 2-6 inches); figure 8 overcast; edge-warp: ivory wool, 6 warps, Z 2 S in 2 bundles of 3 warps each
Ends: ivory wool, plain weave; bottom has no kilim, top has braided fringe
Handle: loose
Colors: blue, ivory, green, goldish brown, dark red, gold, dark brown, dark blue
Condition: low in some areas
Provenance: acquired in Albuquerque, New Mexico, 1972
Published: Bergstrom Art Center 1979, fig. 19

Collection of
Mr. and Mrs. Allen C. West

58

Turkish Kurdish Kilim
Hakkari Tribe
Mid-20th century

This kilim consists of two joined pieces of unequal widths. The field pattern of wide vertical columns with hooked devices and lozenges on blue, ivory and red grounds is typical of kilims from the Hakkari area south of Lake Van. Such kilims, known in the trade as Van kilims, tend to have colors in the dark range, to be wide for their length and to have distinctive macramé and long, dyed fringes. They can be seen wrapped around bedding on the porches of houses in the Hakkari area. The unusually heavy warps in this piece produce a distinctive corduroy effect.

Size: 86 x 61 in./218 x 155 cm.
Warp: wool, Z 2 S; some warps are faded pink and others are tan and ivory plied
Weft: wool, Z 2 S, 35-40 per inch
Edges: ground weft forms a figure 8 around 2 bundles of 2 warps each
Ends: macramé and knotted warp bundles with long fringe
Handle: stiff and heavy
Colors: dark blue, ivory, maroon, orange, light blue, bluish green, brown
Condition: excellent
Provenance: acquired in Van, 1973, from a trader who bought it in the Hakkari area
Published: Landreau 1973, 29, fig. 7; Landreau, ed., 1978, pl. 39

Collection of Ralph S. Yohe

59

Turkish Kurdish Flat-woven Cover
Late 19th century

This outstanding cover (Turkish *cicim*) is composed of four separate panels of plain flat weave in light green, red, dark blue, and orangish red sewn together and decorated with weft float brocading. The patterns are multicolored abstract flowers, ''S''-shapes and hourglass shapes. Both edges of each panel have border designs of zigzags and diamonds between parallel stripes.

Size: 144 x 66 in./366 x 168 cm.
Warp and weft: ground warp and weft of light green, red, blue, and orangish red wool, Z 2 S, in 4 panels; supplemental weft brocading and weft twining in wool and white cotton
Ends: green, red, blue, and orangish red wool plain weave, simple fringe; chain stitching at end not original
Handle: loose
Colors: light green, red, dark blue, orangish red, medium blue, white, purple, yellow
Condition: excellent
Provenance: private collection of flat weaves c. 1900; inventory of Archie Chamalian, New York, c. 1930; acquired by David Chapman, Chicago, c. 1960; by present owner, late 1970s
Published: Landreau and Pickering 1969, fig. 74; Art Institute of Chicago 1973, no. 32

Collection of Joseph W. Fell

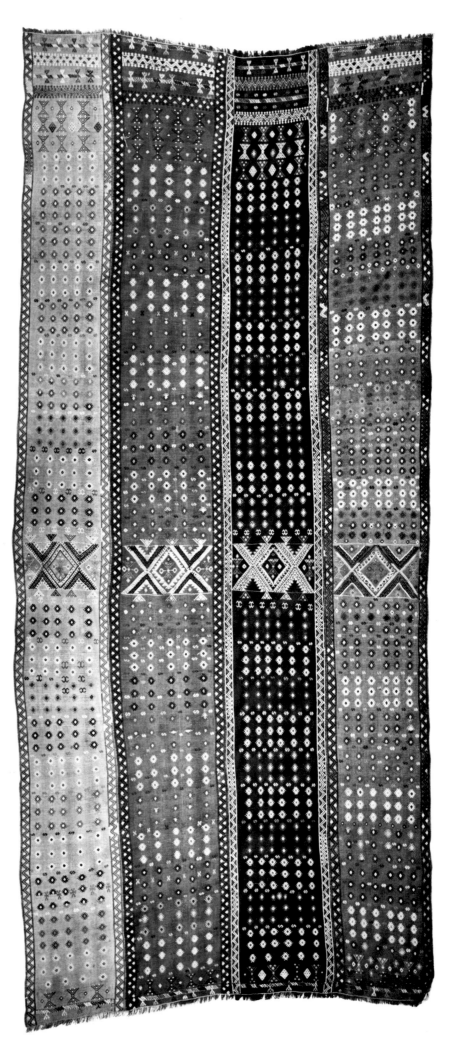

60

Turkish Kurdish Bag
Early 20th century

The lustrous wool accentuates the rectangular pattern of blue and red stars with white centers surrounded by red and blue geometric shapes on a gold ground. The back has bands of red and brown wool plain weave decorated with red and green weft twining, supplemental weft patterning and diamond and "X"-forms in an undulating pattern. The closure loops of red and green braids are attached to the back with weft twine and the closure slits are between panels in various colors. There are bands of weft float patterning and weft twining bordering the closure slit panels.

Size: 40 x 20 in./102 x 51 cm.
Pile: lustrous wool, Z 2 S, symmetrical knot, medium, vert. 9 x horiz. 8 (72 knots per sq. in.)
Warp: ivory wool, Z 2 S, medium offset
Weft: red wool, Z spun, 2 shots
Edges: red wool, single whip; edgewarp: ivory wool, cabled
Ends: red wool plain weave, hemmed
Handle: loose
Colors: gold, red, green, ivory, dark blue, light brown, dark brown, purple
Condition: excellent, browns corroded
Provenance: private collection, Chicago, acquired between 1910 and 1935; by present owner in the Chicago trade, 1977

Private collection

61

Turkish Kurdish Mat
Early 20th century

This mat is almost square with a checkerboard field, the compartments of which are separated by white and orange. The compartments have combinations of blue and red, light green and dark brown, orange and red, green and red, white and light brown. The main border is composed of serrated lozenges and hourglass motifs in the same variety of color combinations. The "running dog" and sawtoothed borders are in light green and dark blue. It is difficult to attribute this mat to a particular area, although the use of figure 8 overcasting identifies it as most likely Kurdish.

Size: 41 x 38 in./104 x 97 cm.
Pile: soft, lustrous wool, Z spun, 2 parallel yarns, symmetrical knot, long, vert. 9 x horiz. 6 (54 knots per sq. in.)
Warp: ivory wool, Z 2 S, no offset
Weft: brown wool, Z spun, 2-3 shots
Edges: wool, orangish red, brown, and tan with a few segments in brown and tan, figure 8 overcasting; foundation weft extends to farthest edgewarp; edgewarp: 2 bundles of 2 ivory wool Z 2 S warps
Ends: orangish red wool, bottom rewoven; line of chain stitching with light blue and reddish orange yarn across the top, loose fringe
Handle: heavy and loose
Colors: red, orange, blue, dark red, ivory, dark brown, black, light green, gray, dark brown
Condition: bottom area rewoven and new fringe added, some repairs to selvedge
Provenance: acquired in Chicago, 1979

Collection of Michael Isberian

62

Turkish Kurdish
Flat-woven Bag
Malatya Area
Early 20th century

In this bag, decorated in the reverse soumak technique, the vivid red and blue, accented by white cotton, make an interesting contrast to the more sedate pile pieces with similar designs. The face has a diamond lattice with white cotton detailing and multicolored angora tufts. The back (incomplete) consists of broad bands of brownish red and dark blue plain weave with supplemental weft decoration in red, blue and white.

Size: 37 x 15 in./94 x 38 cm.
Warp: ivory wool, Z 2 S, 20 per inch
Weft: 20-22 rows of soumak per inch with blue Z spun wool, single shot
Edges: plain
Ends: blue wool, Z spun, plain weave
Handle: coarse
Colors: dark blue, medium blue, greenish blue, dark purple, salmon, brownish red, brown, very dark brown (some yarns wrapped with metal)
Condition: excellent, side stitching missing
Provenance: formerly collection of Dennis R. Dodds; acquired by present owner, 1976

Collection of Maury Bynum

63

**Turkish Kurdish
Flat-woven Bag**
Malatya Area
Early 20th century

This bag is unusual because it is made in the "stocking weave" technique, a fine, discontinuous soumak weave without ground wefts in which supplemental wefts float back and forth. The top and bottom have bands with small red and blue diamonds on an ivory ground. The back has stripes in red, blue and purplish red in plain weave.

Size: 21½ x 23 in./55 x 58 cm.
Warp: brown wool, Z 2 S, 16 per inch
Weft: 32 rows of soumak per inch
Edges: white wool, multiple bundles of warps within supplemental pattern wefts
Ends: red wool plain weave, hemmed, with closure loops; at the bottom of the bag is a band of dark blue and red plain weave columns
Back: 16 warps, 72 wefts per inch
Handle: loose and heavy
Colors: dark red, dark blue, ivory, purplish red, plum, orangish red, yellow, medium blue
Condition: good
Provenance: acquired in Istanbul, 1973
Published: Acar 1975, 39; Landreau, ed., 1978, pl. 27

Collection of Ralph S. Yohe

64

Turkish Kurdish Flat-woven Spindle Bag
Malatya Area
Mid-20th century

In this rare piece, an ivory band separates multicolored alternating triangles containing diamond shapes. The back has bands of blue, plum and red. For a similar example, see Acar 1975, 49.

Size: 9 x 30 in./23 x 76 cm.
Warp: brown goat hair, Z 2 S, across the short dimension of the bag, 13 per inch, no offset
Weft: brown wool ground weft on front and back, 56 per inch; supplemental weft pattern on front in Z 2 S wool and gold-colored metal threads; front of bag has 16 pattern wefts per inch
Edges: blue, red and plum wool; the opening of the bag is embroidered; the other end is plain weave
Ends: red wool plain weave at top, brown hem at bottom
Handle: stiff, heavy
Colors: red, ivory, light green, orangish red, gold, dark blue, fuchsia, dark brown
Condition: excellent
Provenance: acquired from a weaver in the village of Ören near Malatya, Turkey, 1973

Collection of Ralph S. Yohe

Many of the following definitions have been taken from or adapted from Peter F. Stone, *Oriental Rug Repair* (Chicago, 1981), with the author's permission.

abrash
A change in color in the field and border due to differences in wool or dye batches. The color change extends across the rug weft-wise.

asymmetric knot
Also known as the Persian or Senneh knot. It may be open to the right or to the left.

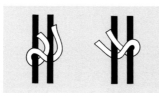

boteh
A pear-shaped figure often used in oriental rug designs. It has been thought to represent a leaf, a bush or a pine cone.

cable weft
When warps are offset or depressed, wefts are alternately straight or bending in their passage through the warps. The straight and tight weft is termed a "cable" weft and the bending weft is termed a "sinuous" weft.

corrosion
The loss of pile in areas of a rug where a dye containing corrosive salts was used. Black or brown dyes are usually involved.

flat weave
A fabric woven without pile.

float
In a plain weave, carrying a weft over two or more adjacent warps or carrying a warp over two or more adjacent wefts.

fringe
Warps extending from the foundation at the end of a rug. These warps are usually treated in a special way (such as macramé) to prevent loss of wefts or pile.

guard border
Stripes or smaller borders used on either side of the main border.

gul
A small medallion of octagonal or angular shape used especially in Turkoman designs.

harshang
Iranian rug design having as its principal motif a shape suggesting a crab (see Edwards 1953, 49).

Herati pattern
The name (derived from the city of Herat) for a design, usually repetitive, consisting of a flower centered in a diamond with curved leaves on each side.

kilim
A flat-woven rug (as distinguished from a pile rug) in which colored wefts are woven back and forth. The term is also used for the flat-weave end of a rug (Persian gilim).

macramé
Off-loom weaving and knot work utilizing the warps at the ends of rugs.

medallion
A large enclosed portion of a design usually located in the center of a field.

"Memling" gul
Medallion motif named after Hans Memling, a fifteenth century Flemish artist whose paintings depict rugs of that design.

mihrab
An arch in an Islamic prayer rug representing the prayer niche in a mosque.

offset
See warp offset.

overcasting
A treatment of the edges of rugs consisting of wrapping or interweaving yarn that is not continuous with the foundation weft.

plain weave
The simplest interlacing of warp and weft in which there is only one weft in each of two sheds composed of alternating warps.

ply
Two or more yarns spun together make a ply or plied yarn.

S spun
Yarn spun in a clockwise direction. The diagonal in the "S" suggests the direction of spin.

selvedge
The edgewarps of a rug and the foundation wefts passing around those warps.

shed
The opening formed through the warps when alternate warps are raised to permit the shuttle and weft to pass through the warps. There is one shed for each set of warps, depending on whether even- or odd-numbered warps are raised.

shot
A weft or the passage of a weft through a shed.

sinuous weft
See cable weft.

skirt
End panel of bag faces and rugs which are outside the main border.

soumak
A flat weave using supplementary wefts in a weft-wrapping technique.

spin
The direction of the twist of yarns; S spun or Z spun.

supplementary weft
A weft that is not structurally essential to a fabric which is added to create a textured or ornamental effect.

supplementary weft float patterning
Ornamentation of a ground fabric with supplementary wefts, continuous from selvedge to selvedge, that skips over two or more adjacent warps.

symmetrical knot
Also known as the Turkish or Giordes knot. It is tied over two warps.

tip fading
Fading of pile ends caused by exposure to light.

vagireh
A sample piece woven to show potential customers various designs (also spelled wagireh).

warp
The yarns running the length of the loom through which the wefts are woven and to which the pile yarns are tied.

warp offset, warp depression
A set of warps can be held in a plane by tight supporting wefts (cable wefts) while alternate warps are permitted to lie in another plane due to loose and bending wefts (sinuous wefts). Alternate warps appear depressed from the back of the rug. Warps may be offset to the extent that one warp may lie on top of another. See cable weft.

weft
Yarns woven through warps by a shuttle. They are the horizontal or crosswise yarns when the fabric is viewed on a loom.

weft-faced
In a balanced plain weave, warps and wefts are equally visible. In a weft-faced fabric, wefts are more closely spaced than warps and the warps are concealed. End kilims are usually weft-faced.

weft float brocade
The use of supplementary wefts, not continuous from selvedge to selvedge, to create a design by skipping over warps.

weft twining
A weft wrapping method in which two wefts pass across warps and twist together after each warp or at regular intervals.

weft wrapping
Any system by which wefts loop around warps rather than only interlacing or passing over and under warps. Soumak is a form of weft wrapping.

Z spun
Yarn spun in a counter-clockwise direction. The diagonal line in the "Z" suggests the direction of spin.

Acar, Belkıs. *Kilim ve düz dokuma yaygılar.* Istanbul: Akbank'ın bir Kültür Hizmeti, 1975.

—————. *Kilim-Cicim-Zili-Sumak: Turkish Flatweaves.* Istanbul: Eren Yayınları, 1983.

Art Institute of Chicago. *Near Eastern Art in Chicago.* Chicago: Art Institute of Chicago, 1973.

Bacharach, Jere L. and Bierman, Irene A. *The Warp and Weft of Islam: Oriental Carpets and Weavings from Pacific Northwest Collections.* Seattle: Henry Art Gallery, University of Washington, 1978.

Ballard, James F. *Catalogue of Oriental Rugs in the Collection of James F. Ballard.* Indianapolis: Hollenbeck, 1924.

Bamborough, Philip. *Antique Oriental Rugs and Carpets.* Poole, England: Blandford Press, 1979.

Benardout, Raymond. *Nomadic Persian and Turkoman Weaving.* London: Raymond Benardout, 1977.

Bergstrom Art Center and Museum. *Oriental Rugs: An Exhibit from Area Collections.* Neenah, Wisc.: John Nelson Bergstrom Art Center and Museum, 1979.

Bidder, Hans. *Carpets from Eastern Turkestan.* New York: Universe Books, 1964.

Cootner, Cathryn. *Flat-woven Textiles: The Arthur D. Jenkins Collection.* Vol. 1. Washington, D.C.: The Textile Museum, 1981.

de Franchis, Amedeo and Wertime, John T. *Lori and Bakhtiyari Flatweaves.* Tehran: Tehran Rug Society, 1976.

Dimand, Maurice S. *The Ballard Collection of Oriental Rugs in the City Art Museum of St. Louis.* St. Louis: City Art Museum of St. Louis, 1935.

Dimand, Maurice S. and Mailey, Jean. *Oriental Rugs in the Metropolitan Museum of Art.* New York: Metropolitan Museum of Art, 1973.

Bands of decorative motifs on an Iraqi Kurdish kilim (detail of cat. no. 43).

Edwards, A. Cecil. *The Persian Carpet*. London: Gerald Duckworth, 1953.

Eiland, Murray L. *Oriental Rugs: A Comprehensive Guide*. Greenwich, Conn.: New York Graphic Society, 1973.

————. *Oriental Rugs: A Comprehensive Guide*. rev. ed. Boston: New York Graphic Society, 1976.

————. *Oriental Rugs: A New Comprehensive Guide*. Boston: Little, Brown and Company, 1981.

Emery, Irene. *The Primary Structures of Fabrics*. Washington, D.C.: The Textile Museum, 1966.

Gans-Ruedin, E. *Modern Oriental Carpets*. London: Thames and Hudson, 1971.

Gardiner, Roger F. *Oriental Rugs from Canadian Collections*. Toronto: Oriental Rug Society, 1975.

Gluck, Jay and Gluck, Sumi, eds. *A Survey of Persian Handicrafts*. Tehran: Bank Melli Iran, 1977.

Görgünay, Neriman. *Doğu yöresi halıları*. [Istanbul ?]: İş Bankası Kültür Yayınları, n.d.

Hawley, Walter A. *Oriental Rugs Antique and Modern*. New York: John Lane, 1913.

Hegenbart, Heinz. *Seltene Webtaschen aus dem Orient*. Munich: Verlag Kunst & Antiquitäten, 1982.

Housego, Jenny. *Tribal Rugs: An Introduction to the Weavings of the Tribes of Iran*. London: Scorpion Publications, 1978.

Iten-Maritz, J. *Turkish Carpets*. Tokyo, New York and San Francisco: Kodansha International, 1977.

Jones, H. McCoy and Boucher, Jeff W. *Baluchi Rugs*. Washington, D.C.: International Hajji Baba Society, 1974.

Jones, H. McCoy; Yohe, Ralph S.; and Boucher, Jeff W. *Persian Tribal Rugs*. Washington, D.C.: Washington Hajji Baba, 1971.

Justin, Valerie S. *Flat-woven Rugs of the World: Kilim, Soumak, and Brocading*. New York: Van Nostrand Reinhold, 1980.

Konieczny, M. G. *Textiles of Baluchistan*. London: British Museum Publications, 1979.

Landreau, Anthony N. "Kurdish Kilim Weaving in the Van-Hakkari District of Eastern Turkey." *Textile Museum Journal* 3, no. 4 (1973): 26-42.

————. ed. *Yörük: The Nomadic Weaving Tradition of the Middle East*. Pittsburgh: Museum of Art, Carnegie Institute, 1978.

Landreau, Anthony N. and Pickering, W. R. *From the Bosporus to Samarkand: Flat-woven Rugs*. Washington, D.C.: The Textile Museum, 1966.

Landreau, Anthony; Yohe, Ralph S.; Bates, Daniel G.; and Landreau, Anita. *Flowers of the Yayla: Yörük Weavings of the Toros Mountains*. Washington, D.C.: The Textile Museum, 1983.

Levine, Louis D. "Notes on Felt-making and the Production of Other Textiles at Seh Gabi, a Kurdish Village." In *Studies in Textile History in Memory of Harold B. Burnham*, edited by Veronika Gervers, 202-213. Toronto: Royal Ontario Museum, 1977.

McMullan, Joseph V. *Islamic Carpets*. New York: Near Eastern Art Research Center, 1965.

————. *Rugs from the Joseph V. McMullan Collection*. Washington, D.C.: Smithsonian Institution, 1966.

Mumford, John K. *Oriental Rugs*. 3d ed. New York: Charles Scribner's Sons, 1902.

Oettingen, R. von. *Meisterstücke orientalischer Knüpfkunst*. 2 vols. Berlin: Scarabaens-Verlag, 1921.

Petsopoulos, Yanni. *Kilims: The Art of Tapestry Weaving in Anatolia, the Caucasus and Persia*. London: Thames and Hudson, 1979.

Saunders, Peter E. *Tribal Visions*. San Raphael, Calif.: Marin Cultural Center, 1980.

Schürmann, Ulrich. *Central-Asian Rugs*. Frankfurt: Osterrieth, 1969.

Stone, Peter F. *Oriental Rug Repair*. Chicago: Greenleaf, 1981.

Wertime, John T. "Flat-woven Structures Found in Nomadic Village Weavings from the Near East and Central Asia." *Textile Museum Journal* 18 (1979): 33-54.

Wulff, Hans E. "Textile Crafts and Leather Crafts." Chap. 4 in *The Traditional Crafts of Persia*. Cambridge, Mass. and London: M.I.T. Press, 1966.

Acknowledgments

ૠ

Many individuals participated in the organization of *Discoveries From Kurdish Looms*. The coordinating committee of the Chicago Rug Society, chaired by McGuire Gibson, included Maury Bynum, Thomas Cook, Barbara Hilpp, Roger Hilpp, Steve Mackey, Linda Sandell, and David Schwartz. Society members serving on the selection committee were Roger Hilpp (chairman), Maury Bynum, Sharon Fenlon, Paul Fong, McGuire Gibson, Michael Isberian, Mary Ann Lea, Steve Mackey, Linda Sandell, and Ralph Yohe. Invaluable assistance was received from each catalogue contributor, particularly William Eagleton, who was able to provide precise origins for a number of pieces.

The arduous task of completing the technical analysis of each rug and weaving benefited from a standardized form developed by Peter Stone. The analyses required many hours of exacting work by the following individuals: Maury Bynum, Michael Cuccello, Roger Hilpp, Steve Mackey, Linda Sandell, David Schwartz, and Peter Stone.

The editing of the technical descriptions and the essays was the responsibility of Robert D. Biggs along with Thomas Cook and David Schwartz. Their thoroughness is evident in the pages that follow. The preparation of the manuscript also benefited from the translations and material provided by Professors Heshmat Moayyad and Helene J. Kantor of the University of Chicago and the assistance of Paula Woods of the *Journal of Near Eastern Studies*. Additional editing and proofreading assistance was provided by Nicole Netter, Aviva Rubin and Suzanne Wise.

Much credit is due Karl Snoblin, Block Gallery registrar and preparator, for the photography for this publication. In addition, his many talents are reflected in the handsome installation of the exhibition at the Block Gallery. Stephanie May, Block Gallery department assistant, and Suzanne Wise, Block Gallery curator, coordinated innumerable details of the exhibition. Publicity was expertly handled by Charlotte Moser of Northwestern University's Department of University Relations. The design and production of this publication were the responsibility of Hayward Blake and Shenaya Bhote along with Kay Fulton and Rhonda Inouye; their creativity and patience are gratefully acknowledged. Special thanks are due Carl Reisig of Congress Printing for his efforts in meeting a seemingly impossible deadline.

The dedication of all those who contributed to the realization of *Discoveries From Kurdish Looms* will long be remembered.

KKF

Colophon

𝜂

Typography: Optima Bold and Regular, Roman and Italic.

Paper: Strathmore Americana, Felt Finish, Cover Basis 80. Warren Lustro Offset Enamel, Cream Dull Finish, Text Basis 100.

Printing: Offset Lithography and Silk-screening.

Design: Hayward Blake & Co.

Photography: Karl Snoblin, cat. nos. 1-8 and 10-64; Kranzten Studio, Chicago, cat. no. 9.

Typography: Black Dot, Inc.

Silk-screening: Proto-Grafix, Ltd.

Printing: Congress Printing Co.

Printed in the United States of America.

ૠ